THE UNOFFICIAL MASTERBUILT®

SMOKER COOKBOOK 2

A BBQ SMOKING GUIDE & 121 ELECTRIC SMOKER RECIPES

SMOKIN' BOB JENSEN

The Unofficial Masterbuilt® Smoker Cookbook 2: A BBQ Smoking Guide & 121 Electric Smoker Recipes

Cooking With A Foodie publishes its books in a variety of digital and print formats. Some content that appears in print may not be available in digital format, and vice versa.

ISBN: Print 978-1-944797-00-3 | Ebook

A PERSONAL INVITATION

Thank you for checking out my book. I think you'll love it.

I'm very grateful to have wonderful readers who support us, so I'm going to extend to you an invitation to join my exclusive club—the Fireside Pit.

This is a brand new offer I created to see whether folks would be interested in seeing more great products from me. It will be like a fireside chat by the barbecue pit.

Once in a while, you will receive incredible promotional offers on top of the line products that either I sell or ones from companies I personally use.

Membership is always free, even if you decide to leave and come back later.

What kind of huge discounts do Fireside Pit Members get?
- Get recipes, secrets and techniques straight from the pros right to your inbox
- My future books for free
- Incredible offers on popular bbq and kitchen products like the one featured below

EXTRA STRONG STAINLESS STEEL GRILLING SET

- ❏ **EXTRA STRONG** — Durable High-Quality Stainless Steel

- ❏ **EASY TO CLEAN** — Dishwasher Safe

- ❏ **INCLUDES EVERYTHING** — Essential BBQ Tools

- ❏ **LIFETIME** Guarantee

**To Get This Product For Up To 50% OFF
Sign Up At fpclub.smokeandgrillmeat.com**

Contents

MEAT BUYING GUIDE

WHERE TO BUY MEAT

Do your best to source meat from places like farmer's markets, butchers, or local co-ops. There is a remarkable difference in the quality of local, organic, free-range meat and poultry.

BEEF

Shopping for beef can be incredibly confusing. Every beginning cook has walked into a supermarket to buy a steak and stood paralyzed in the meat case, staring at package after package of beautiful meat, asking themselves what a "chuck tender steak" is. And every beginning cook has, at some point, walked out of the supermarket with the wrong cut of meat for their preparation. Rather than continue to make costly mistakes, check out this handy beef-buying guide for your next barbecue.

BEEF CUTS AND OTHER BASIC BEEF TERMS

Before we start, let's get a few definitions out of the way.

- Primal cuts - In butchering, primal cuts are pieces of meat that are separated from the carcass during butchering.
- Subprimal cuts - Subprimal cuts are made by butchers to break down the larger cuts into more usable pieces. If the loin is the primal cut, the tenderloin would be a subprimal cut.
- Forequarter - Cuts of meat that come from the front of the cow
- Hindquarter - Cuts of meat that come from the back of the cow

PRIMAL CUTS OF BEEF

		Also Known As
Forequarter Cuts	Chuck or shoulder	Bone-in chuck steaks and roasts (arm or blade), and boneless clod steaks and roasts
	Rib	Short ribs, the prime rib and rib-eye steaks
	Brisket	Corned beef or pastrami
	Shank	Used primarily for stews and soups; also used in ground beef
	Plate	Short ribs, Pot roast, and Skirt steak. Also used in ground beef, as it is typically a tough and fatty meat.
Hindquarter cuts	Loin	• Short loin, from which the T-bone and porterhouse, or strip steaks are cut. • Sirloin, which is less tender than short loin, but more flavorful. This can be further divided into top sirloin and bottom sirloin (including tri-tip). • Tenderloin, which is the most tender. It can be removed as a separate subprimal, and cut into filet mignons, tournedos or tenderloin steaks, and roasts (such as for beef Wellington). They can also be cut bone-in to make parts of T-bone and porterhouse steaks.
	Round	Round steak, eye of round, top round, and bottom round steaks and roasts.
	Flank	Flank steak, London broil, and skirt steak.

CLASSIFICATION OF BEEF ACCORDING TO GRADE

Once upon a time, you had to rely on your butcher's word when examining the quality of your meat. Today, the U.S. Department of Agriculture (USDA) classifies quality into three categories: prime, choice, and select. This grading system not only applies to beef but for most meats such as pork and lamb.

Meat Grade According to the USDA	Characteristics	Availability	Cost
Prime	• Has several marble streaks (like "veins") • Tender • Flavorful	• High-end butcher shops • Specialty restaurants	• Twice the price of choice meats, but depends on the cut
Choice	• With some marble streaks on meat • Somewhat tender • Acceptable flavor	• Local meat shops and supermarkets	• Relatively affordable given the quality, but depends on the cut
Select	• With slight marble streaks on meat • Tough • More on the bland side	• Local meat shops and supermarkets	• Cheapest among the three grades of meat

LABELING BASICS AND OTHER TERMS EXPLAINED

Recently consumers have become more interested in where their meat comes from. In response, producers have begun labeling their products with terms such as "grain-fed" or "organic". However, the USDA no longer regulates what beef can be labeled as "grass-fed", so paying more may not always yield a better product. Your best bet is to patron a trusted butcher who knows where his product is raised.

Common Labels	Characteristics	Pros	Cons
Grain-Fed Beef	• Tends to be dark in color • Contains more fat • Has a milder flavor	• The streaks of intramuscular fat in grain-fed beef contributes to the mildly rich flavor of the meat.	• Lower in omega-3 fatty acids • Grain is used by farmers to supplement a cow's diet, but has an affect on the overall quality of its meat.
Grass-Fed Beef	• Contains less fat • Chewy texture • Has a gamey odor • Strong, complex flavor	• The meat has less intramuscular fat due to the nature of the animal's diet, thus, the meat is more on the chewy side and has a strong, pungent flavor and odor. • Has a broader range of beneficial fats and nutrients not found in grain-fed meat	• The pungent flavor may turn off some people. • Grass-fed beef tends to be more expensive than grain-fed beef.
Organic	• Raised without antibiotics or hormones • Animals live in conditions that accommodate their ability to graze on pasture • Fed 100% organic feed • Has a "USDA Organic" seal	• The "USDA Organic" seal ensures farmers have adhered to strict guidelines for raising these animals.	• Can be a little pricier than regular meats in the market.
Blade, mechanically or needle tenderized	• Meat has been passed through a machine that punctures it with small, sharp needles or blades to break the connective tissues and muscle fibers that results in a more chewy, tender cut.	• Blade-tenderized beef cuts when cooked tend are indeed more tender (when cooked at 160 degrees)	• The blades and needles used to tenderize the beef may transfer disease-causing bacteria such as E. coli. To counter this contamination, make sure to cook the beef to a safe temperature of 160 degrees.

BUYING BEEF BY CUT

Now that you are thoroughly familiar with the labels on those glorious packages of beautiful meat, it's time to get down to the nitty gritty. What cut do you use for smoking? Braising? Grilling?

PRIMAL CUTS OF BEEF AND OTHER CUTS

1. Beef Primal Cut: Chuck or Shoulder

Shoulder Steak

Characteristics: Relatively lean with a mild beef flavor

Flavor: 2/5
Tenderness: 2/5
Cost: $
Other name/s: Chuck steak
Recommended Cooking Method: Grilling
Notes & Tips: After cooking, meat should be thinly sliced on a bias.

Top Blade Roast

Characteristics: A boneless, flat cut with a mild flavor, which can sometimes be substituted for a chuck-eye roast.

Flavor: 3/5
Cost: $$
Other name/s: Chuck roast, first cut, blade roast, top chuck roast
Recommended Cooking Method: Braising, stewing
Notes & Tips: Top blade roasts reach their maximum flavor with long, slow, moist cooking. Try using this cut for your next pot roast for succulent meat and outstanding gravy.

Blade Steak

Characteristics: a small shoulder cut that has a rich flavor and is very tender

Flavor: 3/5
Tenderness: 3/5
Cost: $
Other name/s: Top blade steak, flat-iron steak
Recommended Cooking Method: Stir-frying, braising, stewing, broiling, grilling
Notes & Tips: Remove the gristle line at the middle of the meat and cut the steak into thin slices for stir-fries. Also makes great kebabs.

Chuck 7-Bone Roast

Characteristics: a cut based from a number seven-shaped bone that has a rich flavor

Flavor: 3/5
Cost: $$
Other name/s: Center-cut pot roast, center-cut chuck roast
Recommended Cooking Method: Braising, stewing
Notes & Tips: When braising, add less liquid than you would a top blade roast as this cut already has a deep flavor.

Chuck-Eye Roast

Characteristics: Boneless roast cut from the center (or "eye") of the first five ribs; extremely tender and juicy due to the abundance of fat in the meat

Flavor: 3/5
Cost: $$
Other name/s: Boneless chuck roll, boneless chuck fillet
Recommended Cooking Method: Braising, stewing, roasting
Notes & Tips: For pot roast, use kitchen twine to handle this cut effectively.

Chuck Shoulder Roast

Characteristics: Mild flavor, not a lot of fat or connective tissue.

Flavor: 2/5
Cost: $$
Other name/s: Chuck shoulder pot roast, boneless chuck roast
Recommended Cooking Method: Braising, stewing.
Notes & Tips: Because of its low cost, chuck shoulder roast makes great stew meat. Cut in smaller chunks, brown the meat and cook slowly with root vegetables.

Under-Blade Roast

Characteristics: Its rich flavor is comparable to the seven bone roast but contains more connective tissue and ample amount of fat.

Flavor: 3/5
Cost: $$
Other name/s: Bottom chuck roast, California roast
Recommended Cooking Method: Braising, stewing, roasting
Notes & Tips: Meat tends to fall apart when carved because of its tenderness.

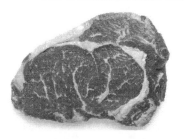
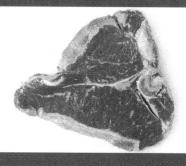

2. Beef Primal Cut: Rib

Rib Steak

Characteristics: A bone-in steak cut from a prime rib roast

Flavor: 3/5
Tenderness: 3/5
Cost: $$$
Other name/s: None
Recommended Cooking Method: Grilling, roasting, barbecuing

Rib-Eye Steak

Characteristics: A rib steak without the bone that has an oval shape and a narrow strip of meat that curves around one end; a beefy, tender and juicy cut of beef.

Flavor: 4/5
Tenderness: 2/5
Cost: $$$
Other name/s: Spencer steak, Delmonico steak
Recommended Cooking Method: Grilling, pan searing, barbecuing

Rib Roast, First Cut

Characteristics: Rib roast cut consisting of ribs 10 through 12 -- which have the big, single rib-eye section with less fat; closer to the loin end

Flavor: 4/5
Cost: $$$$
Other name/s: Prime rib, loin end, small end
Recommended Cooking Method: Grill roasting, roasting, barbecuing

Rib Roast, Second Cut

Characteristics: A rib roast cut consisting of ribs 6 to 8 or 9, which contains more intramuscular fat that adds flavor into the roast

Flavor: 4/5
Cost: $$$$
Other name/s: Large end
Recommended Cooking Method: Roasting, barbecuing

Beef Ribs

Characteristics: large rib cut from bones 6 to 12 of the prime rib, which are about 8 inches long and perfect for barbecuing

Flavor: 3/5
Cost: $$
Other name/s: Back ribs
Recommended Cooking Method: Barbecuing
Notes & Tips: Usually sold as a big slab of rib, but some retailers offer smaller cuts with just 3-4 bones per slab.

3. Beef Primal Cut:Short Loin

Strip Steak

Characteristics: A cut that runs along the shell muscle in the center of the steer's back; it is well marbled, has a tight grain with a strong beefy taste and a satisfying chewy texture

Flavor: 4/5
Cost: $$$
Tenderness: 3/5
Other name/s: Shell steak, top loin steak, sirloin strip steak, New York Strip steak, Kansas City strip steak
Recommended Cooking Method: Grilling, pan searing

Tenderloin

Characteristics: The most tender cut of beef with a mild, almost non-beefy flavor

Flavor: 1/5
Cost: $$$$
Other name/s: Whole fillet, Chateaubriand
Recommended Cooking Method: Grilling, roasting
Notes & Tips: Unpeeled varieties of this cut come with a big layer of exterior fat that should be removed prior to cooking.

For peeled varieties, the fat is seen distributed throughout the cut and may be left as is.

T-Bone Steak

Characteristics: A cut named after the T-shaped bone that appears through the meat. The bone separates two different cuts of meat - the tenderloin on the right and the strip on the left.

Flavor: 4/5
Cost: $$$
Tenderness: 3/5
Other name/s:
Recommended Cooking Method: Grilling, pan searing

Porterhouse Steak

Characteristics: A large T-bone steak with a bigger cut of tenderloin than a traditional T-Bone steak. It has a well-balanced texture and flavor like the T-bone steak.

Flavor: 4/5
Cost: $$$
Tenderness: 3/5
Other name/s: None
Recommended Cooking Method: Grilling, pan searing

Filet Mignon

Characteristics: A cut from the narrow end of the tenderloin that is 1-2 inches thick. Filet Mignon has a very mild beef flavor and a pleasantly tender texture

Flavor: 1/5
Cost: $$$$
Tenderness: 4/5
Other name/s: Chateaubriand, tenderloin steak, tournedo
Recommended Cooking Method: Grilling, pan searing
Notes & Tips: Because people tend to value texture over flavor, tenderloin is among the most expensive cuts of beef you can buy. It also goes by a few different names.

Chateaubriand is a center-cut steak cut from the largest part of the tenderloin, around 3 inches thick; it is big enough for two servings.

Tournedos are the smallest tenderloin cuts that come from the section toward the tip end of the tenderloin, around 1 inch thick only.

4. Beef Primal Cut: Sirloin

Sirloin Tri-Tip Roast

Characteristics: a small, triangular-shaped roast with a gentle flavor and moist, spongy texture.

Flavor: 2/5
Cost: $$
Other name/s: Triangle roast
Recommended Cooking Method: Grilling, barbecuing
Notes & Tips: Tri-tip is a popular beef cut among West Coast butchers. East Coast butchers turn this cut into sirloin tips, or "steak tips".

5. Beef Primal Cut: Round

Cube Steak

Characteristics: A chewy cut of meat without a lot of fat or connective tissue.

Flavor: 1/5
Tenderness: 1/5
Cost: $
Other name/s: Minute steak
Recommended Cooking Method: Cube steaks are best when pounded with a meat tenderizer and pan seared. This cut is most popularly used for chicken fried steak.

Top Round Steak

Characteristics: A cut with a pleasant beefy taste and chewy texture.

Flavor: 3/5
Tenderness: 2/5
Cost: $
Other name/s: Inside round cut, London broil
Recommended Cooking Method: Broiling, grilling
Notes & Tips: To reduce the chewiness of this steak, cook it to medium doneness and slice it super thin.

Bottom Round Rump Roast

Characteristics: A cut that is slightly less tender than the top round roast; juicy and has a mild flavor when cooked.

Flavor: 2/5
Cost: $
Other name/s: Bottom round oven roast, bottom round pot roast, round roast
Recommended Cooking Method: Roasting

Top Round Roast

Characteristics: A cut similar to the top sirloin roast which has a good texture, flavor, and juiciness.

Flavor: 3/5
Cost: $
Other name/s: Top round steak roast, top round first cut
Recommended Cooking Method: Roasting
Notes & Tips: Upon serving, cut this roast into thinner slices as it tends to become chewy when sliced thick.

Eye-Round Roast

Characteristics: A boneless cut that slices nicely, the eye-round roast can be as flavorful as other top cuts with proper treatment.

Flavor: 2/5
Cost: $
Other name/s: Round-eye roast
Recommended Cooking Method: Grilling, barbecuing
Notes & Tips: Because this roast reaches its maximum tenderness in a low-heat oven, barbecuing this roast to a medium doneness is ideal. Be sure to slice it thin when serving.

Bottom Round Roast

Characteristics: Because it doesn't have a distinct flavor of its own, bottom round roasts are ideal for stewing and braising.

Flavor: 1/5
Cost: $
Other name/s: None
Recommended Cooking Method: Braising, stewing
Notes & Tips: Braise or stew the bottom round roast in flavorful liquid. A combination of red wine and beef broth would be nice.

6. Beef Primal Cut: Brisket, Shank, Plate, Flank

Skirt Steak

Characteristics: A thin cut from the underside of the cow with more fat content than flank steak.

Flavor: 3/5
Tenderness: 3/5
Cost: $$$
Other name/s: Philadelphia steak, fajita steak
Recommended Cooking Method: Grilling, stir-frying, pan searing
Notes & Tips: Before cooking, remove the silverskin on the back of the steak for maximum tenderness. Grill quickly over a high heat and thinly slice across the grain for maximum tenderness.

Flank Steak

Characteristics: A wide, flat cut from the underside of the animal bearing a recognizable longitudinal grain.

Flavor: 3/5
Tenderness: 3/5
Cost: $$$
Other name/s: Jiffy steak
Recommended Cooking Method: Grilling, stir-frying, pan searing
Notes & Tips: This steak is quite thin for its size, so it cooks quickly.
Flank steak should never be cooked past medium doneness.
Always thinly slice the steak across the grain, with a heavy bias.

Hanger Steak

Characteristics: The hanger steak refers to the large muscle near the diaphragm on the underside of the cow that hangs down the center of the animal (thus the name hanger steak).

Flavor: 3/5
Tenderness: 1/5
Cost: $$
Other name/s: Butcher's steak, hanging tender, hanging tenderloin
Recommended Cooking Method: Grilling, pan searing
Notes & Tips: Hanger steak is around a third of the price of tenderloin with a lot more flavor.
Be sure to have your butcher remove all of the excess fat and silver skin that typically surrounds this cut of meat.

Brisket

Characteristics: a large steak with a rectangular shake that weighs approximately 13 pounds and is further cut into 2 sub cuts: flat and point cuts.

Flavor: 3/5
Cost: $$
Other name/s: None
Recommended Cooking Method: Braising, barbecuing
Notes & Tips: The flat cut brisket is a thinner, leaner cut good for slow cooking.

If smoking is the name of the game, you will want a brisket with a nice fat cap on top to keep the meat moist.

Shank

Characteristics: A cut derived from the cross-section of the front leg with a rounded shape; a fatty, but tasty cut.

Flavor: 2/5
Cost: $
Other name/s: Center beef shank
Recommended Cooking Method: Braising
Notes & Tips: This cut is available with or without the bone in.

The shank is equivalent to the osso buco of a calf's meat.

It is good to use in soups or simmered dinner recipes like pot-au-feu.

Short Ribs

Characteristics: A meaty cut that is usually taken from the underside of the cow (but can be cut in various parts, too) with each rib bone detached and cut crosswise.

Flavor: 3/5
Cost: $
Other name/s: English-style short ribs
Recommended Cooking Method: Stewing, braising, barbecuing

Flanken-Style Short Ribs

Characteristics: similar to the English-style short ribs, but are cut thinly into cross sections with 2-3 meaty bone pieces.

Flavor: 3/5
Cost: $$
Other name/s: Flanken
Recommended Cooking Method: Barbecuing, braising
Notes & Tips: These short ribs are more rare than the English style short ribs, but are generally sold in butcher shops.

Meat Facts:

- The leanest cuts of meat from four-legged animals almost always come from the loin. Look for words like sirloin or tenderloin

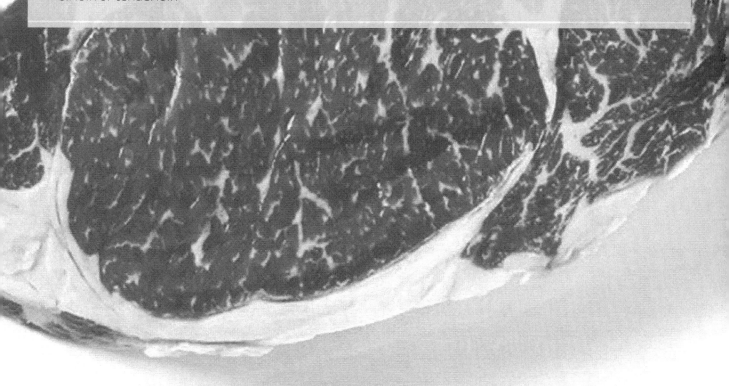

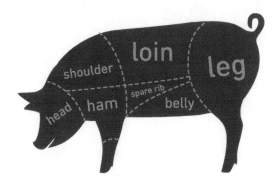

PORK

Once upon a time, American society really only ate pork for breakfast. Chicken was considered healthy, beef was thought to be luxurious, and pork was made into ham and bacon and the occasional pork chop. Thought to be too fatty to be eaten on a regular basis, ordinary citizens went about their days ignoring the thousands of ways pork could be transformed into delicious dishes.

Modern breeding systems and feeding techniques over the years created pigs with a third less fat than their porcine ancestors. Ingenious marketing in the early 1990s brought pork into American consciousness as "the other white meat" and just like that, pork became a relatively inexpensive, delicious, versatile protein addition to our daily diet.

Just like beef, there are a lot of different cuts and retailer labels for pork. Using our handy guide, you can become an expert pork purchaser.

LABELING

Heritage Breeds

Over the last decade, consumers have become more aware of how their pork is being raised and the effect the life of the animal has on the meat. The term "Heritage Breeds" has recently come into vogue when describing pork products, but what does it actually mean? According to The Livestock Conservancy, in order for pork to be labeled as a "Heritage Swine", it must be a true genetic breed of swine that has had a continuous breeding population in the US since 1925. However, the term "Heritage Breeds" when referring to meat is not USDA regulated and therefore open to interpretation.

For some farmers, heritage breed pork is a general term for meat from livestock that are raised as they would have been hundreds of years ago. Animals are allowed to feed on grass and grain and are raised without artificial hormones.

For other farmers, heritage breed pork comes from breeds common to the Americas hundreds of years ago, such as Berkshire and Duroc. The idea behind the propagation of heritage breeds is that they considerably more flavorful than their commercial counterparts and they protect the species as a whole. If all pigs were of one breed, a particularly nasty and widespread disease could wipe out the entire pork production industry.

While the USDA does not regulate the term "heritage breed pork", a high quality butcher who has a relationship with his farmers will be able to direct you to higher quality, more flavorful cuts of meat.

Quality and pH Level

According to Kenneth Prusa, Food Science professor at the Iowa State University, the color of pork is a strong indication of quality. Pork meat from both Berkshire and Duroc breeds have a vibrant pink to red tint to them (although Duroc isn't as red as the crimson-colored Berkshire breed of pork), which indicates that the meat has a higher pH than their supermarket pork counterparts. Prusa added that pH is the "overall driver of quality in pork." Hence, the higher the pH of the pork, the better the quality of the pork.

In fact, just a small difference in the pH level of pork greatly affects the texture and flavor of the meat. Berkshire breeds are strategically raised to have a little higher pH level than normal pigs; the normal pH for mammals is approximately 7. In effect, the slightly higher pH of Berkshire breeds makes the meat firmer, tastier a deeper red. Also, Prusa added that the pH level is more significant than the fat content of the pork in terms of assessing the flavor of the meat.

Factors Affecting pH Level

Husbandry. Berkshire pigs are grown in an environment with minimal stress. It is believed that when the animal experiences less stress and is more relaxed, its blood flows more evenly. This results in flavorful juices distributed well into its system.

Slaughtering methods. When Berkshire pigs are scheduled to be slaughtered, they are also subjected to little stress so that there wouldn't be a buildup of lactic acid in the muscles that results to a lower pH. The quality of the animal's last few days can greatly affect the final quality of the flavor and texture of its meat. Obviously, animals raised naturally are the least likely to be subject to high-stress environments like being locked in cages.

Blast chilling. Another way to avoid decreasing the pH level of the meat is by blast chilling it immediately after slaughter. It is important to note that once blood flow stops, the pH level of the meat rapidly decreases, so blast chilling it helps preserve the higher pH level of the pig.

ENHANCED PORK

Since regular pigs found in supermarkets are leaner and less flavorful than their heritage breed counterparts, many meat suppliers use flavor-enhancing meat injections to improve the overall flavor of modern pork.

Sodium Solution
Enhanced pork products are injected with sodium solution to improve the flavor of the meat. The solution is a mixture of water, salt,

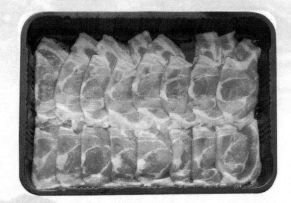

potassium lactate, sodium phosphates, sodium diacetate, sodium lactate, and other flavor-enhancing agents. Such an enhancers are often used in leaner cuts like loin and tenderloin to add flavor to an otherwise bland cut.

While sodium solution injections enhance the flavor of the pork, they do so at a price. Pork injected with a flavor-enhancing solution weighs 7-15 percent more than unenhanced pork products. As a result, the flavor tends to be salty and leave a spongy texture when it is cooked. Also, enhanced pork tends to lose almost six times its moisture content when frozen and thawed.

Nitrite and Nitrate Content
Nitrites and nitrates are food preservatives that fight bacteria in processed or cured meats. They are also the compounds that give meat its deep pink color. Both compounds are typically found in the brine of cured pork products such as ham, bacon, and lunch meat. Celery juice is often used as an alternative to chemical preservatives because of its naturally high nitrate content.

These compounds are generally considered safe to consume, although nitrites and nitrates have been linked to migraine headaches in some individuals. Even if pork products are labeled as "nitrite- or nitrate-free", these compounds are usually present in a natural form as a result of the curing process.

PRIMAL CUTS OF PORK

Pork is broken down into four initial series of cuts, more commonly known as "primal cuts" -- which include the shoulder, side or belly, loin, and leg. These primal cuts are wholesale items from the butcher level and are then sold in various cuts by supermarkets and local meat shops.

PRIMAL CUTS OF PORK

1. Shoulder

There are two basic portions from this cut of pork, -- the blade shoulder and picnic shoulder:

Blade shoulder - Cut from the upper section of the pork shoulder, a blade shoulder is evenly marbled with fat and holds a lot of connective tissue. Cuts from this portion of the pork shoulder are typically used for slow cooking methods like stewing, braising and barbecuing.

Picnic shoulder - Cut from the section near the front leg area of the pig. Cuts from this portion of the pork shoulder are quite similar to the cuts from the blade shoulder, but are considered to be more economical.

2. Side or Belly

As the name suggests, this portion contains the most fat of all of the cuts from the underside of the animal. This primal cut is where the spare ribs and bacon cuts are taken.

3. Loin

The cut from the section between the shoulder and the back legs is called the loin. It is the leanest and most tender part of the pig.

Popular cuts found in this area include loin chops, rib chops, loin roasts, and tenderloin roasts. Because of their lack of fat, it is important to cook them with a meat thermometer as they can become dry and lose flavor if overcooked.

4. Leg

The legs at the back of the animal are usually referred to as "ham". They are often sold as large roasts in fresh or cured varieties.

SHOPPING FOR PORK

At the supermarket or local meat shop level, each primal cut is sold in a variety of other cuts and under a litany of different labels. This handy guide will ensure you are familiar with the kind of cut you need before heading to the nearest supermarket or butcher.

1. Primal Cut: Shoulder

Pork Shoulder

Characteristics: Contains a lot of fat and connective tissue; sold either bone-in or boneless

Flavor: 4/5
Cost: $
Other name/s: Fresh picnic roast, picnic roast, picnic shoulder, shoulder arm picnic roast
Recommended Cooking Method: Braising, roasting, grill roasting, barbecuing

Pork Butt Roast

Characteristics: Big cut weighing up to 8 pounds; can be sold with the bone in; has an excellent flavor

Flavor: 4/5
Cost: $$
Other name/s: Boston butt, Boston shoulder, pork butt
Recommended Cooking Method: Stewing, braising, slow roasting, barbecuing
Notes & Tips: This roast can be sold in smaller cuts and is usually packaged in a mesh netting that holds the roast together.

2. Primal Cut: Side or Belly

St. Louis Style Spareribs

Characteristics: This style of cut uses whole ribs near the belly area of the animal; weighs about 5 pounds or more, as it consists of the brisket bone and meat.

Flavor: 4/5
Cost: $$$
Other name/s: Spareribs
Recommended Cooking Method: Barbecuing, roasting
Notes & Tips: A popular cut for barbecuing because it can be easily managed on a grill or smoker. The connective tissue and fat on St. Louis style spareribs keep the meat moist during long, slow cooking.

3. Primal Cut: Loin

Rib Chop

Characteristics: A cut taken from the rib area of the loin and has a recognizable bone running along one side and a big eye of loin muscle; these chops are fatty and juicy as long as they are not overcooked.

Flavor: 3/5
Cost: $$$
Other name/s: Pork chops end cut, rib cut chops
Recommended Cooking Method: Braising, roasting, pan searing, grilling
Notes & Tips: Rib chops can be sold boneless.

Blade Chop

Characteristics: A cut taken from the shoulder end of the loin, which contains a lot of fat and is quite tough; has a porky, pleasant flavor and is juicy

Flavor: 3/5
Cost: $$$
Other name/s: Pork chop end cut
Recommended Cooking Method: Braising, barbecuing

Center-Cut Chop

Characteristics: A chop with a distinct bone that divides the tenderloin muscle from the loin meat; contains less fat than rib chops, but have a mild pork flavor

Flavor: 2/5
Cost: $$
Other name/s: Loin chops, top loin chops
Recommended Cooking Method: Grilling, searing
Notes & Tips: Cooking this chop can be challenging since the tenderloin portion tends to cook faster than the loin section.

Sirloin Chops

Characteristics: a chop cut from the sirloin or the hip end of the pig containing a piece of the hipbone, tenderloin, and loin meat.

Flavor: 2/5
Cost: $
Other name/s: Sirloin steaks
Recommended Cooking Method: Pan searing, braising, barbecuing

Baby Back Ribs

Characteristics: Cut from the area of the rib cage nearest to the backbone, these ribs are smaller and leaner than spareribs.

Flavor: 3/5
Cost: $$$$
Other name/s: Riblets, loin back ribs
Recommended Cooking Method: Barbecuing, braising
Notes & Tips: Ribs benefit from low and slow cooking. Combine braising and smoking for optimum texture and flavor.

Country-Style Ribs

Characteristics: A boneless rib cut from the side just above the rib cage, from the blade end of the loin; the meat is tender with a rich flavor.

Flavor: 3/5
Cost: $$
Other name/s: Country ribs
Recommended Cooking Method: Grilling, braising, pan searing, barbecuing
Notes & Tips: Most butchers cut this type of ribs into several cuts and then place them in a single package.

Blade End Roast

Characteristics: The section of the loin nearest to the shoulder; it can be challenging to carve, as it has a lot of different fat pockets and muscles on the meat.

Flavor: 3/5
Cost: $$
Other name/s: Rib-end roast, pork five-rib roast, pork loin rib end, pork seven-rib roast
Recommended Cooking Method: Roasting, braising

Boneless Blade End Roast

Characteristics: A cut from the shoulder end of the loin; fatty, and more flavorful than the boneless center-cut loin roast.

Flavor: 2/5
Cost: $$
Other name/s: Triangle roast
Recommended Cooking Method: Grilling, roasting
Notes & Tips: It may be quite difficult to find this type of cut in most meat shops.

Center-Cut Loin Roast

Characteristics: A cut similar to the boneless blade-end roast that can also be juicy and tender.

Flavor: 2/5
Cost: $$$
Other name/s: Center-cut pork roast
Recommended Cooking Method: Grill roasting, roasting
Notes & Tips: Buy this roast with a nice fat cap on top and cook it with the fat cap on top. This allows the meat to self-baste and stay moist.

Center-Cut Rib Roast

Characteristics: A cut consisting of five to eight ribs with the bones and fat still encased within the meat; it has a good flavor and slightly tender texture similar to the prime rib or rack of lamb.

Flavor: 3/5
Cost: $$$$
Other name/s: Center-cut pork roast, pork loin rib half, rack of pork
Recommended Cooking Method: Grilling, roasting

Tenderloin Roast

Characteristics: A very small cut of meat that is boneless and lean with very little marbling; this cut is equivalent to beef tenderloin.

Flavor: 1/5
Cost: $$$
Other name/s: None
Recommended Cooking Method: Pan searing, sauteing, stir-frying, roasting

Sirloin Roast

Characteristics: A cut with lots of connective tissue, making it ideal for braising and barbecuing.

Flavor: 1/5
Cost: $$
Other name/s: None
Recommended Cooking Method: Braising, barbecuing
Notes & Tips: Sirloin roasts are ideal for slow cooking. For maximum flavor, be sure to marinate or rub prior to cooking.

Crown Roast

Characteristics: A cut from two bone-in center-cut rib or center-cut loin roasts attached together, usually containing 16 to 20 ribs.

Flavor: 3/5
Cost: $$$$
Other name/s: Crown rib roast
Recommended Cooking Method: Roasting
Notes & Tips: A crown rib roast is very impressive when served whole. Because of its shape and size, it is important to work with a meat thermometer to prevent overcooking.

Fresh Ham (Shank End)

Characteristics: The first cut derived from the leg area is the shank end, which is covered with a thick layer of skin and fat.

Flavor: 3/5
Cost: $$
Other name/s: Shank end fresh ham
Recommended Cooking Method: Roasting, barbecuing
Notes & Tips: The fatty layer in this cut is just enough to keep the meat juicy and this cut will actually become more flavorful if you brine or marinate it first. Be sure to score the skin prior to brining or marinating to allow the liquid to penetrate the meat.

Fresh Ham (Sirloin Half)

Characteristics: The second cut derived from the leg of the animal with a rounded shape because of the bone structure; a flavorful cut, but may be difficult to carve because of its shape.

Flavor: 3/5
Cost: $
Other name/s: None
Recommended Cooking Method: Roasting, barbecuing
Notes & Tips: Like its shank end cousin, this ham will take on the flavor of whatever marinade or brine you apply to it. Just be sure to purchase it with the skin on and score the skin prior to marinating.

Spiral-Sliced Bone-in Half Ham

Characteristics: A wet-cured ham that is flavorful and easy to cut; a bone-in ham is tastier than a boneless ham since the bone also develops its flavor as it cooks.

Flavor: 4/5
Cost: $
Other name/s: Spiral-cut ham
Recommended Cooking Method: Roasting
Notes & Tips: Buy the bone-in ham with the label "ham with natural juices".

Prepared hams also benefit from a slow reheating process making them ideal for parties or events.

Country Ham

Characteristics: A whole leg that is dry-cured with a salty, nutty flavor.

Flavor: 3/5
Cost: $$$
Other name/s: None
Recommended Cooking Method: Pan searing after slicing
Notes & Tips: It is important to think of country ham like prosciutto. It is delicious on its own, but very pungent. Ideally, country ham is served as a condiment rather than a main course. Top biscuits with very thin slices or use in place of prosciutto in pastas.

LAMB

Unlike beef and pork, lamb has typically been called the less popular option when buying meat. More recently, however, it has surged in popularity for three good reasons: price, taste, and versatility of cooking. Lamb is comparably more affordable than beef, and has a stronger flavor than pork. It can also be prepared using a variety of cooking methods, making it ideal for grilling, roasting, or even braising.

Consumers can buy domestic or imported lamb depending on the desired product. American lamb is larger and milder than lamb imported from New Zealand or Australia. The main reason for this difference is the diet the animals are fed. Imported lamb are grass-fed, usually on various grasses, while American lamb is raised on a mixed diet of grass and grain.

Often, lamb sold in supermarkets has been slaughtered at between six to twelve months old, to give the meat a mild flavor that consumers are accustomed to. If the animal is slaughtered as an adult, its meat will be labeled as mutton and will have a tough texture and gamey flavor ideal for braising and stewing.

PRIMAL CUTS OF LAMB

A lamb is divided into five major primal cuts that are then cut into smaller sections. Each cut has a recommended cooking method and varies in cost.

PRIMAL CUTS OF LAMB
Breast or Foreshank This cut consists of the underside portion of the animal: foreshank and breast.   This includes the two front legs/shank, and the breast portion.
Shoulder This lamb section runs from the neck through the fourth rib of the animal. Because these muscles are worked a lot during the animal's life, this cut tends to be tough but flavorful making it ideal for braising and stewing.
Rib This area covers the section directly behind the shoulder from the fifth rib to the twelfth rib. All eight ribs from this portion are collectively called a rack. When the rack is cut into individual pieces, they are called rib chops, which have a fine, tender grain and pleasant flavor.
Loin This cut starts from the last rib and extends down to the hip area. The loin is considered to be the most popular cut, due to its tender texture and mild flavor, similar to the rib chops.
Leg This portion starts from the hip down to the hoof of the animal. Consumers can buy them whole or cut into smaller roasts and shanks (from the two back legs).   They can also be bought bones in, boneless, or butterflied.

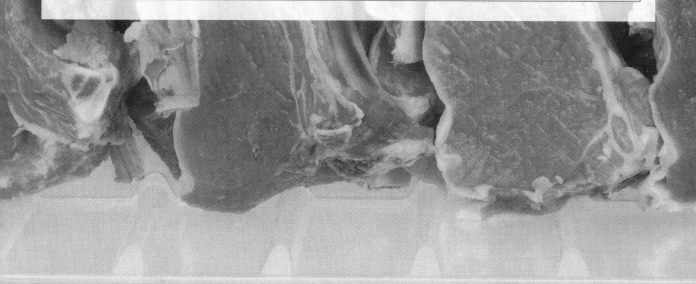

SHOPPING GUIDE FOR LAMB

If you haven't had lamb lately, now is the time to give it a try. Its unique flavor and varying texture naturally lends itself to a variety of cooking methods. It can be more expensive than other cuts of meat and purchasing the wrong cut can lead to a costly mistake on the barbecue. This handy guide will keep you on the right track when buying your next piece of lamb.

1. Primal Cut: Foreshank or Breast

Characteristics: Cut derived from the underside of the animal which includes the breast and the two front legs.

Flavor: 3/5
Cost: $$$$
Other name/s: None
Recommended Cooking Method: Roasting, grilling

2. Primal Cut: Shoulder

Blade Chops

Characteristics: A cut derived from the shoulder area, it has a thin part of the blade bone and a part of the chine or backbone; it contains more fat than round-bone chops but are pleasantly chewy and have a robust flavor.

Flavor: 3/5
Cost: $$
Other name/s: Shoulder chops
Recommended Cooking Method: Grilling, pan searing

Round-Bone Chops

Characteristics: Oval cuts taken from the shoulder portion; leaner than blade chops, these chops have a strong, lamby flavor.

Flavor: 3/5
Cost: $$
Other name/s: Arm chops
Recommended Cooking Method: Grilling, braising
Notes & Tips: Every round-bone chop consists of a cross section of the arm bone similar to a small ham steak and a small line of riblets of both sides of the chop.

3. Primal Cut: Loin

Loin Chops

Characteristics: A cut which contains meat from either side of the bone running down the center of the loin; it has a stronger lamb flavor than the rib chops and are firm, but not chewy.

Flavor: 4/5
Cost: $$$$
Other name/s: None
Recommended Cooking Method: Grilling, pan searing
Notes & Tips: The small piece of meat at the right side of the loin chop bone is fine-grained and comparably tender to the tenderloin of a pig or cow. The larger piece of meat on the other side of the loin chop bone is more chewy.

4. Primal Cut: Rib

Rib Chops

Characteristics: A cut that has a recognizable bone on one side of the chop. Rib chops usually have a lot of fat, especially near the bone; ribs chops have a refined, slightly sweet taste and a tender texture.

Flavor: 4/5
Cost: $$$$
Other name/s: Frenched chops, rack chops
Recommended Cooking Method: Pan searing, grilling, roasting
Notes & Tips: If you want leaner rib chops, you can ask the butcher to "french" or scrape the fat away from the tip of the bone, and thus the alternate name "Frenched chops".

To get the best results, do not cook these chops past medium-rare for a mildly sweet flavor.

Rack of Lamb

Characteristics: A cut that consists of eight to nine bones; this cut is very tender and flavorful comparable to the prime rib of a cow.

Flavor: 4/5
Cost: $$$$
Other name/s: Rib roast, rack roast
Recommended Cooking Method: Roasting

5. Primal Cut: Leg

Leg of Lamb

Characteristics: A cut derived from the wider sirloin end and the narrower shank end consisting of the butt end (sirloin or hip meat) and the shank end or ankle at the bottom part of the animal; it usually weighs six to ten pounds and is ideal for a variety of preparations.

Flavor: 3/5
Cost: $$$
Other name/s: Sirloin-on leg, whole leg
Recommended Cooking Method: Grilling, barbecuing, roasting, braising

Notes & Tips: A leg of lamb is ideal for marinades and rubs. Ask your butcher to bone and butterfly the leg if you are looking to grill this cut to a medium rare. For braises, the lamb leg can be stuffed, rolled, and tied. Or barbecue the whole leg, bone and all, for a tasty treat.

POULTRY

Poultry is the most popular meat in the U.S. because of its low cost and pleasant flavor. As consumers have become more aware of where their poultry comes from and how it is raised, new cooks may be confused by the variety of labels on their chicken or turkey.

LABELING

POULTRY PACKAGING TERMS THAT YOU SHOULD KNOW

USDA Organic
In order to be labeled as "USDA Organic", farmers have to adhere to guidelines set forth by the USDA for the care, feeding, and slaughtering of poultry animals. Animals must be raised on an organic feed diet without animal byproducts, antibiotics, or growth hormones. They must be given year-round access to the outdoors, shade, shelter, and clean water. Any bedding must be made from organic materials and shelters must allow for adequate exercise and normal behaviors.

Raised Without Antibiotics
The term "Raised Without Antibiotics" is a marketing term and is not regulated by the USDA. It generally means that animals were not given any medications classified as antibiotics for disease prevention or treatment. Since the USDA requires that an animal treated with antibiotics cannot be slaughtered until the substance has left the animal's system, all poultry is technically antibiotic free when it reaches the market.

Hormone-Free
"Hormone-Free" is also a marketing term used on poultry packaging. Contrary to popular belief, the USDA prohibits the use of steroids or hormones in all poultry or pork production. Companies that use "hormone-free" labeling are free to do so, but it is not indicative of a better quality product than poultry without the designation.

Natural and All Natural
The USDA requires that poultry products carrying these labels have no artificial ingredients, artificial colors or chemical preservatives. However, "natural" and "all natural" labels still allow for the injection of sodium solutions to enhance the flavor of the product.

Vegetarian-Fed and the Vegetarian Diet
The USDA has no specific regulation regarding this claim. Traditional poultry feed is made from corn and soybean meal but may be enhanced with protein, fats, and oils from animal byproducts. Farmers may choose to use a feed that does not contain animal products, but chickens are not naturally vegetarians. Wild birds consume a diet rich in insects and other small creatures in addition to seeds and plant matter.

Air-Chilled
"Air-chilled" poultry products refer to the way the meat was treated after slaughter. In the US, most poultry is chilled in large, chlorinated ice water baths before packaging. While this process is fast, it also uses a tremendous amount of water, dilutes the poultry's flavor, and causes the finished product to weigh more due to water retention. Air-chilling poultry is a much slower process, where the product is hung individually on a conveyor belt and circulated around a chilling room. Not only is it more environmentally friendly, it results in a more flavorful final product.

Free Range
The only USDA requirement for a poultry producer to label its product as "free range" or "free roaming" is that the animal has access to the outside. Unfortunately, this does not guarantee that the flavor or quality of the meat be grossly affected in any way.

SHOPPING GUIDE FOR POULTRY

Chicken and turkey is generally easier to shop for than beef, pork, or lamb. However, there are still some factors to consider when buying poultry products.

CHICKEN

Types of Chicken Packaging

Whole: Roasters, Broilers, and Fryers

Whole chickens come in three varieties: roasters, broilers and fryers.

Roasters - Older chickens that typically weigh between five to seven pounds.

Broilers and fryers - Younger chickens that weigh between 2 ½ to 4 ½ pounds.

Avoid labels that say the chicken is "enhanced". This means it may contain unnecessary "flavor enhancers" that may affect the flavor and texture of the chicken. Not to mention, you are actually paying for the water solution they inject the chicken with. Buy birds labeled "air chilled" or "USDA Organic" for the most flavorful chicken.

Ground

Ground chicken in supermarkets is prepared in one of two ways: prepackaged or ground to order.

Prepackaged - ground chicken meat from either dark or white meats

Ground to order - ground meat from buyer's choice of chicken

Because chicken must be cooked thoroughly, choosing ground chicken with a large amount of dark meat will yield a juicier, more flavorful end product.

Boneless, Skinless Breasts and Cutlets

Boneless, skinless breasts and cutlets are the most popular cuts in the US. Lean, versatile, and neutral in flavor, they are a staple in households throughout the country. Just be sure to use a meat thermometer when cooking them as they become dry and rubbery when they are overcooked.

Next time, give boneless, skinless chicken thighs a try in place of the breasts. They are packed with chicken flavor and won't dry out as quickly.

Bone-In Parts

Chefs generally agree that roasting chicken with the bone in and skin on will yield the juiciest, most flavorful outcome.

Bone-in, skin-on parts are ideal for the barbecue or grill.

TURKEY

Types of Turkey Packaging

Whole

Most whole turkeys available in the market today do not contain as much fat as they did fifty years ago, leaving the birds dry and flavorless.

Heritage birds are purebred or cross bred descendants of wild turkeys that roamed freely decades ago. These turkeys have a rich flavor and texture but may be difficult to find in a supermarket.

To combat the lack of flavor in traditional birds, some processors "prebaste" the turkey with a sodium solution to improve the flavor. It is always better to buy a bird that has not been injected with water and brine it yourself. Not only can you control the ingredients in the brine, you do not pay for the additional weight of the sodium solution.

Bone-In Breasts

Bone-in breasts found in supermarkets are available in two varieties:

(1) Regular or True Cut
(2) Hotel or Country-Style

Regular or True Cut

The cut which includes the whole bone-in breast section with ribs and parts of the wing meat, back, and neck skin.

Hotel or Country-Style

This cut is basically the same as regular turkey breast, except that it comes with the neck, wings, and giblets.

Ground

When buying ground turkey, be sure to buy a variety that contains a mixture of white meat and dark meat for extra flavor and added juiciness.

The Sad Truth

■ Most of the meat in the United States is produced industrially. Cramped living conditions, artificial diets, and growth hormones are utilized in many facilities to produce more livestock or poultry for consumption. Unfortunately, this affects the quality of the meat you find in the supermarket. Your best bet is to befriend a trusted butcher who sources his products from local farmers. Not only are you supporting your local agricultural industry, you will have access to high quality meat and poultry raised in more humane conditions.

Woodchip Guide

Pellets and chunks are not recommended for the Masterbuilt® Electric Smokers, but any kind of wood chips can be used. However, look for a wood chip that matches your desired level of smoke.

Wood	Level of Smoke	Ideal For:
Alder	Light, sweet	Chicken and fish
Fruit Woods (Cherry, apple, peach, plum)	Light, sweet	Poultry, fish, and pork.
Pecan	Light to medium	Any meat, fish, poultry
Hickory	Medium, rich flavor	Any meat, fish, poultry
Maple	Medium, sweet	Vegetables, poultry, fish, or pork.
Oak	Medium to strong	Pork, beef, lamb
Walnut	Strong	Beef or lamb, but may overpower chicken or fish.
Mesquite	Strong	Beef or lamb, but may overpower chicken or fish.

Is It Done Yet?

Every chef will tell you that, when it comes to cooking meat, temperature matters more than time. Investing in a high quality meat thermometer will ensure thousands of successful roasts, steaks, briskets, and chickens for decades to come. But how do you know when your meat is ready?

First, it is important to understand a little about what happens to meat at different temperatures.

Temperature	What Happens to Meat
0°F (-18°C)	Ideal freezer temperature.
25°F (-4°C)	Meat freezes. Since the water in meat contains proteins, meat freezes at a lower temperature than plain water.
32°F (0°C)	Water freezes.
34-39°F (1-4°C)	Water is not frozen and microbial growth is minimized making this the ideal refrigerator temperature.
41-135°F (5-57°C)	The USDA refers to this as the "danger zone" for bacterial growth. At these temperatures, bacteria can double in as little as 20 minutes increasing the likelihood of food-borne illness.
95-130°F (35-54°C)	Animal fat starts to melt.
120°F (49°C)	Myosin, the protein involved in muscle contraction, begins to lose its structure in a process called "denaturing".
130°F (54°C)	Many pathogens begin to die, slowly. At this temperature it takes over two hours to pasteurize meat, meaning all of the pathogenic bacteria is dead.
130-135°F (54-57°C)	Medium rare doneness. Fats begin to render, or liquefy, albeit slowly.
140°F (60°C)	Collagen begins to contract pushing pink juice from the muscle fibers onto the surface of the meat. Red or pink juices begin to turn clear and bead up on the surface of the meat.
150°F (66°C)	The muscle protein actin begins to denature making the meat tough and dry.
150-165° (66-74°C)	When you are cooking large cuts of meat, such as pork butt or beef brisket, this is what is known as "the stall zone". Meat seems to get stuck in this temperature range for hours because moisture evaporates on the surface of the meat and cools it like sweat. Once evaporation slows, the meat's temperature will start to rise again.
160-165°F (71-74°C)	The "instant kill zone". Most meat is safe to eat long before this temperature because the majority of the bacteria is on the surface. However, in the case of ground meats, it is necessary to cook them beyond well done in order to ensure their safety.
160-205°F (71-96°C)	Tough collagens melt and form tender gelatin. Dehydrated fibers begin to fall apart and pull away from any bones and the meat is easy to shred.

Temperature Guide

To accurately test the temperature of your meat, insert an instant-read meat thermometer into the thickest portion. For poultry, this will be the meatiest part of the thigh, being careful not to touch the bone. If your smoker is equipped with a temperature probe, by all means, use it. This will not only prevent heat from escaping the smoker, it will give you a digital reading throughout the cooking process.

Cut of meat	Desired Internal Temperature
BEEF	
Brisket	190-200°F (190°F for sliced, 200°F for pulled)
Chuck Roast	190-200°F
Ribs	185-190°F
Short Ribs	190-200°F
Beef Country Style Ribs	175-180°F
Meatloaf	160°F
Burgers	160°F
Steaks	135°F (Medium Rare), 145°F (Medium)
Prime Rib	130-135°F (Medium Rare)
Tri Tip	130-135°F (Medium Rare)
PORK	
Pork Butt	205°F
Baby Back Ribs	180°F
Spare Ribs	180-185°F
Loin	145°F
Tenderloin	145°F
POULTRY	
Whole Chicken	165°F
Chicken Legs/Thighs	165°F
Chicken Wings	165°F
Chicken Quarters	165°F

Whole Turkey	165°F
Turkey Breast	165°F
Turkey Legs	175-180°F
Quail/Pheasant	165°F
Cornish Hens	165°F

FISH & SEAFOOD

Salmon	145°F
Tilapia	145°F
Whole Trout	145°F
Lobster Tails	140°F
Oysters	Oysters that have been shucked, rinsed, and smoked in a shell half are done when the edges start to curl.
Scallops	145°F
Shrimp	Shrimp are done when they turn bright pink and opaque.

MISCELLANEOUS

Sausages	175°F
Corn on the cob	Cook until kernels change color
Whole potatoes	Cook until soft
Tomatoes	Cook until skin splits

PANTRY STOCKING GUIDE

Every pitmaster will tell you that a well-stocked pantry is the key to success. However, what that pantry consists of will vary according to your tastes. Here are a few basics every cook should have to ensure their barbecue comes out spectacular very time.

Spices
- Kosher salt (It dissolves quickly, doesn't have a metallic flavor, and is the favorite of chefs everywhere.)
- Black pepper (Bonus for peppercorns that can be freshly ground)
- Brown sugar
- White sugar
- Paprika
- Chili powder
- Red chili flake
- Garlic powder
- Onion powder
- Dried thyme
- Allspice
- Celery seed
- Dry mustard
- Cayenne pepper

Canned Goods
- Tomato sauce
- Tomato puree
- Diced tomatoes
- Tomato paste
- Beer
- Apple juice

Sauces
- Mustard
- Soy sauce
- Ketchup
- Worcestershire sauce
- Extra Virgin Olive Oil
- Your favorite hot sauce (try sriracha, sambal, or Thai sweet chili sauce for a flavorful twist)
- Apple cider vinegar (Most bottles of apple cider vinegar are actually colored white vinegar. Pay a little extra for real apple cider vinegar for a better flavor.)
- Honey or Maple syrup
- Mayonnaise
- Molasses

Aromatics
- Onions
- Lemons or Limes
- Garlic

AWESOME RUBS, MARINADES, MOPS & SAUCES

Rubs

Adobo Rub
Asian Rub
Basic Barbecue Rub
Basic Beef Rub
Berbere Spice Mix
Big Bold Barbecue Rub
Cajun Dry Rub
Carne Asada Rub
Chile Rub
Classic American Brown Sugar Dry Rub
Coffee Dry Rub
Country Style Dry Rub
Dry Rub For Pork
English Pub Rub
Garlic Lover's Rub
Grill Seasoning
Habanero Rub
Indian Spice Rub
Kansas City Dry Rub
Malaysian Rub
Mama's Barbecue Rub
Mediterranean Spice Rub
Money Rub
North African Rub
Paprika Herb Rub
Rosemary Garlic Rub
Salt and Pepper Steak Rub
Spicy Tunisian Rub
Sweet and Savory Dry Rub
Tuscan Spice Rub

Marinades, Mops & Sauces

Balsamic Barbecue Sauce
Barbecue Beef Mop
Beer Mop for Brisket
Blueberry Barbecue Sauce
Chinese Barbecue Sauce (Char Sui)
Chipotle Mango Lime Barbecue Sauce
Classic Texas Barbecue Sauce
Cola Barbecue Sauce
Coffee Spice Barbecue Sauce
East Carolina Barbecue Sauce
Everything Basting Sauce
Frank's Buffalo Sauce
Honey Chipotle Barbecue Sauce
Jeff Phillips' Mop Water
Kansas City Barbecue Sauce
Memphis Barbecue Sauce
Memphis Mop
Peach Mustard Barbecue Sauce
Peanut Sauce
Quick Barbecue Sauce
Southern Barbecue Sauce
St. Louis Barbecue Sauce
Sweet and Sour Barbecue Sauce
Texas Hillbilly Mop Sauce
White Barbecue Sauce

RUBS

Adobo Rub

Ingredients:
- ❏ 1 Tablespoon (Tbsp) ancho chili powder
- ❏ 1 teaspoon (tsp). ground cumin
- ❏ 1 tsp onion powder
- ❏ 1 tsp garlic powder
- ❏ 1 tsp salt
- ❏ ½ tsp pepper
- ❏ The juice of 1 lime
- ❏ 2 Tbsp extra-virgin olive oil

Thoroughly combine ingredients in a small bowl and rub on chicken or pork. Allow to sit for 4-6 hours or overnight before smoking.

Asian Rub

Ingredients:
- ❏ ¼ c paprika (Spanish or sweet paprika works best)
- ❏ 2 Tbsp dry mustard
- ❏ 2 Tbsp Chinese Five Spice Powder
- ❏ 2 Tbsp ground ginger
- ❏ 1 Tbsp salt
- ❏ 1 Tbsp pepper
- ❏ 1 Tbsp crushed red pepper flakes

Combine all ingredients in a small bowl. May be stored in an airtight container for up to 6 months.

> TIP: Once you have mastered a few rubs, try adding new ingredients to see what new combinations you can come up with. Tomato powder, green chile powder, or even smoked orange zest are all available through online retailers and make delicious additions to a basic barbecue rub.

Basic Barbecue Rub
(Also known as 4-3-2-1 rub)

The idea behind this versatile rub is really just the proportions. 4 parts salt, 3 parts sugar, 2 parts paprika, and 1 part of one or several spices.

Basic Ingredients:
- ❏ 4 Tbsp salt
- ❏ 3 Tbsp brown sugar
- ❏ 2 Tbsp paprika
- ❏ 1 Tbsp cayenne powder

Combine ingredients in a small bowl. Rub onto meat and skin and allow to sit at least one hour before smoking. Unused portions can be kept in an airtight container for up to 6 months.

For ribs, try brown sugar, smoked paprika, and 1 Tbsp each garlic powder, onion powder, chili powder, black pepper, and cayenne pepper.

Basic Beef Rub

This rub contains no salt, but rather relies on a hefty kick from black and cayenne peppers for a powerful flavor.

Ingredients:
- ❏ 3 Tbsp coarsely ground black pepper
- ❏ 1 Tbsp white sugar
- ❏ 1 Tbsp onion powder
- ❏ 2 tsp dried mustard
- ❏ 2 tsp garlic powder
- ❏ 2 tsp chili powder
- ❏ 1 tsp cayenne pepper

Combine ingredients in a small bowl. Rub onto meat and skin and allow to sit at least one hour before smoking. Unused portions can be kept in an airtight container for up to 6 months.

Berbere Spice Mix

This sweet and spicy rub is perfect for chicken or pork to give it a Middle Eastern flair.

Ingredients:
- ❏ 1 Tbsp paprika
- ❏ 1 ½ tsp cayenne pepper
- ❏ 1 ½ tsp ground ginger
- ❏ 1 tsp ground allspice
- ❏ 1 tsp ground cumin
- ❏ ½ tsp nutmeg
- ❏ ½ tsp ground cinnamon
- ❏ ½ tsp dried oregano
- ❏ ¼ tsp ground cloves

Combine ingredients in a small bowl. Rub onto meat and skin and allow to sit at least one hour before smoking. Unused portions can be kept in an airtight container for up to 6 months.

Big Bold Barbecue Rub

Sweeter than most, the heat in this rub is offset somewhat by the sugar.

Ingredients:
- ❏ ½ cup brown sugar
- ❏ 1/4 c sweet paprika
- ❏ 1 Tbsp ground black pepper
- ❏ 1 Tbsp lemon pepper
- ❏ 1 Tbsp kosher salt
- ❏ 1 Tbsp chili powder
- ❏ 1 Tbsp garlic powder
- ❏ 1 Tbsp onion powder
- ❏ 1 Tbsp cayenne pepper

Combine ingredients in a small bowl. Rub onto meat and skin and allow to sit at least one hour before smoking. Unused portions can be kept in an airtight container for up to 6 months.

Cajun Dry Rub

Cajun doesn't always mean super spicy. Although this rub has a fair amount of heat, the herbs serve to bring a little something extra to the party.

Ingredients:
- ❏ 2 Tbsp Kosher salt
- ❏ 2 Tbsp sweet paprika
- ❏ 2 tsp dried thyme
- ❏ 2 tsp dried oregano
- ❏ 2 tsp black pepper
- ❏ 2 tsp granulated garlic
- ❏ 2 tsp dried onion
- ❏ 1 tsp cayenne pepper
- ❏ 1 bay leaves, ground

Combine ingredients in a small bowl. Rub onto meat and skin and allow to sit at least one hour before smoking. Unused portions can be kept in an airtight container for up to 6 months.

Carne Asada Rub

In Latin America, "carne asada" literally means "grilled meat". While the flavors in the rubs and marinades for carne asada vary, this zippy rub adds a Latin flare with very few ingredients. This is a wet rub and should be made no more than a day in advance.

Ingredients:
- ❏ 2 cloves garlic, crushed
- ❏ 2 Tbsp lime juice
- ❏ 2 Tbsp orange juice
- ❏ 2 Tbsp extra-virgin olive oil
- ❏ 1 Tbsp lime zest
- ❏ 1 Tbsp orange zest
- ❏ 1 tsp ancho chili powder
- ❏ 1 tsp cumin
- ❏ 1 tsp salt
- ❏ ½ tsp pepper
- ❏ ½ tsp Mexican oregano

Combine in a small bowl. Slather on the meat and allow it to sit at least 30 minutes before smoking or grilling.

Chile Rub

Ingredients:
- ❏ 4 dried New Mexico chiles
- ❏ 4 dried guajillo chiles
- ❏ 4 dried ancho chiles
- ❏ ½ c cumin seeds
- ❏ ¼ c dried oregano
- ❏ ¼ c paprika
- ❏ 3 Tbsp kosher salt

Combine all ingredients into a spice grinder and pulse until thoroughly ground. Then add:
- ❏ 1 Tbsp onion powder
- ❏ 2 tsp garlic powder

Combine ingredients in a small bowl. Rub onto meat and skin and allow to sit at least one hour before smoking. Unused portions can be kept in an airtight container for up to 6 months.

Classic American Brown Sugar Dry Rub

This sweet and smoky rub is exactly what you imagine a Kansas City style rub to be.

Ingredients
- ❏ ½ cup light brown sugar
- ❏ ¼ c smoked paprika
- ❏ 4 Tbsp kosher salt
- ❏ 3 Tbsp black pepper
- ❏ 2 tsp onion powder
- ❏ 2 tsp garlic powder
- ❏ 2 tsp celery seed
- ❏ 1 tsp red pepper flakes

Combine ingredients in a small bowl. Rub onto meat and skin and allow to sit at least one hour before smoking. Unused portions can be kept in an airtight container for up to 6 months.

Coffee Dry Rub

This rub is a strong, slightly bitter addition to any piece of beef or pork.

Ingredients:
- ❏ 3 Tbsp ground coffee
- ❏ 2 Tbsp dark brown sugar
- ❏ 1 Tbsp kosher salt
- ❏ 1 Tbsp paprika
- ❏ 1 Tbsp black pepper
- ❏ ½ tsp ground coriander

Combine ingredients in a small bowl. Rub onto meat and skin and allow to sit at least one hour before smoking. Unused portions can be kept in an airtight container for up to 6 months.

Country Style Dry Rub

The addition of celery seed gives this rub a floral background perfect for chicken and fish

Ingredients:
- ❏ 1 c white sugar
- ❏ ½ c kosher salt
- ❏ ¼ c sweet paprika
- ❏ 2 Tbsp garlic powder

- ❏ 1 Tbsp ground cumin
- ❏ 1 Tbsp cayenne pepper
- ❏ 1 Tbsp black pepper
- ❏ 1 tsp ground celery seed

Combine ingredients in a small bowl. Rub onto meat and skin and allow to sit at least one hour before smoking. Unused portions can be kept in an airtight container for up to 6 months.

Dry Rub For Pork

This recipe makes a lot of rub.

Ingredients:
- ❏ ¼ cup light brown sugar
- ❏ ¼ cup kosher salt
- ❏ ¼ cup paprika
- ❏ 2 Tbsp black pepper
- ❏ 2 Tbsp garlic powder
- ❏ 2 Tbsp onion powder
- ❏ 1 Tbsp cayenne pepper

Combine ingredients in a small bowl. Rub onto meat and skin and allow to sit at least one hour before smoking. Unused portions can be kept in an airtight container for up to 6 months.

English Pub Rub

This rub is ideal for steak of any kind. The beef bouillon enhances the steak flavor while the aromatics send the flavor to a whole new level.

Ingredients:
- ❏ 1 beef bouillon cube, pulverized
- ❏ 2 cloves garlic, crushed
- ❏ 1 small shallot, finely diced
- ❏ 1 tsp kosher salt
- ❏ ¼ c extra-virgin olive oil

Combine ingredients in a small bowl and slather on the steaks. Allow to sit at least 30 minutes before smoking.

Garlic Lover's Rub

This rub is for the garlic lover in all of us. It's so versatile you can use it on any piece of meat, seafood, poultry, or vegetable.

Ingredients:
- ❏ 8 cloves garlic, minced
- ❏ 1 Tbsp extra-virgin olive oil
- ❏ 2 tsp dijon or stone-ground mustard
- ❏ 1 tsp kosher salt
- ❏ ½ tsp black pepper
- ❏ The zest of one lemon
- ❏

Combine ingredients in a small bowl and slather on your protein of choice at least 30 minutes before smoking.

Grill Seasoning

While there are delicious grill seasonings on the market, they are so easy to make and customize to your taste, why not make it yourself?

Ingredients:
- ❏ ¼ c kosher salt
- ❏ ¼ c black pepper
- ❏ 2 Tbsp granulated garlic
- ❏ 2 Tbsp granulated onion
- ❏ 1 Tbsp cracked coriander seeds

Combine ingredients in a small bowl. Rub onto meat and skin and allow to sit at least one hour before smoking. Unused portions can be kept in an airtight container for up to 6 months. Also try:
- Substitute coriander seeds for dehydrated lemon zest and ground fennel seed for a great chicken rub.
- Add ground celery seed for a bright, floral flavor

Habanero Rub

This jerk-inspired rub is sweet, spicy, and super flavorful. It can be made as a dry rub as written, or as a wet rub by blending the first nine ingredients with a chopped habanero chile, the juice of one lime, and ¼ cup of extra-virgin olive oil. Either way, break out the flip flops and sunglasses because you're headed to the Caribbean.

Ingredients:
- ❏ 3 Tbsp onion powder
- ❏ 2 Tbsp garlic powder
- ❏ 2 Tbsp paprika
- ❏ 2 Tbsp light brown sugar
- ❏ 1 Tbsp ground allspice
- ❏ 1 Tbsp ground chipotle chile powder
- ❏ 2 tsp ground cinnamon
- ❏ 2 tsp ground thyme
- ❏ 1 tsp ground habanero chile powder
- ❏ 1 tsp ground dried lemon peel
- ❏ ½ tsp ground nutmeg

Combine ingredients in a small bowl. Rub onto meat and skin and allow to sit at least one hour before smoking. Unused portions can be kept in an airtight container for up to 6 months.

Tip: You can find habanero chile powder online, but if you are in a pinch, substitute cayenne pepper and increase the dried lemon peel to 1 ½ tsp

Indian Spice Rub

Ingredients:
- ❏ 6 Tbsp curry powder
- ❏ 3 Tbsp kosher salt
- ❏ 1 Tbsp crushed red pepper flakes
- ❏ 1 Tbsp ground cumin
- ❏ 1 Tbsp ground coriander
- ❏ 2 tsp turmeric
- ❏ 2 tsp ground ginger
- ❏ 1 tsp garam masala

Combine ingredients in a small bowl. Rub onto meat and skin and allow to sit at least one hour before smoking. Unused portions can be kept in an airtight container for up to 6 months.

Tip: Garam masala is the northern India equivalent of "chili powder" in the US. It is a combination of spices that varies from one brand to another and is readily available in supermarkets. It is also commonly used in the Indian dishes khorma and tikka masala.

Kansas City Dry Rub

Kansas City style barbecue is known for sweet rubs and sweet, tomato-based sauces without a lot of heat. This recipe makes a lot of rub for easy access to delicious barbecue flavor for months to come.

Ingredients:
- ❏ 1 cup brown sugar
- ❏ 1 cup white sugar
- ❏ ¼ c paprika
- ❏ ½ c kosher salt
- ❏ 2 tsp black pepper
- ❏ 2 tsp chili powder
- ❏ 2 tsp garlic powder
- ❏ ½ tsp cayenne pepper

Combine ingredients in a small bowl. Rub onto meat and skin and allow to sit at least one hour before smoking. Unused portions can be kept in an airtight container for up to 6 months.

Malaysian Rub

Malaysian cooking is known for balancing four things - salt, sour, bitter, and sweet. This rub reflects that sensibility. If you cannot find lemongrass at your Asian market, substitute zest and juice of one lemon and 3 Tbsp of chopped flat leaf parsley.

Ingredients:
- ❏ 1 Tbsp fish sauce
- ❏ 2 Tbsp fresh grated ginger
- ❏ 2 Tbsp lemongrass, minced
- ❏ 1 Tbsp turmeric

- ❏ 1 Tbsp sugar
- ❏ 2 cloves garlic, crushed
- ❏ 2 limes, zested and juiced

Combine ingredients in a small bowl. Slather on meat, chicken or fish and allow to sit for at least 30 minutes before smoking.

Mama's Barbecue Rub

There isn't an actual mama behind this recipe, but you can imagine it, right?

Ingredients:
- ❏ ¼ cup paprika
- ❏ 2 Tbsp chili powder
- ❏ 2 tsp Kosher salt
- ❏ 1 tsp dry mustard
- ❏ ½ tsp onion powder
- ❏ ½ tsp garlic powder
- ❏ ½ tsp dried basil

Combine ingredients in a small bowl. Rub onto meat and skin and allow to sit at least one hour before smoking. Unused portions can be kept in an airtight container for up to 6 months.

Mediterranean Spice Rub

This rub will remind you of oceanside afternoons in Greece. This is perfect as a dry rub on chicken, fish, or lamb, or can be made as a wet rub with fresh herbs, fresh garlic, and ¼ cup extra-virgin olive oil.

Ingredients:
- ❏ 3 Tbsp dried rosemary
- ❏ 2 Tbsp ground cumin
- ❏ 2 Tbsp ground coriander
- ❏ 1 Tbsp dried oregano
- ❏ 2 tsp ground cinnamon
- ❏ 2 tsp garlic powder
- ❏ 1 tsp kosher salt

Combine ingredients in a small bowl. Rub onto meat and skin and allow to sit at least one hour before smoking. Unused portions can be kept in an airtight container for up to 6 months.

Money Rub

Named for the phrase "right on the money", the addition of lemon pepper to this rub gives it a zesty zip, perfect for chicken or seafood.

Ingredients:
- ❏ ¼ c chili powder
- ❏ 2 Tbsp paprika
- ❏ 2 Tbsp black pepper
- ❏ 1 ½ Tbsp lemon pepper
- ❏ 1 Tbsp onion powder
- ❏ 1 Tbsp garlic powder
- ❏ 1 tsp cayenne pepper

Combine ingredients in a small bowl. Rub onto meat and skin and allow to sit at least one hour before smoking. Unused portions can be kept in an airtight container for up to 6 months.

North African Rub

Harissa paste is a spicy chile paste. If you cannot find it, you can substitute sriracha or sambal.

Ingredients:
- ❏ 2 Tbsp chili powder
- ❏ 1 Tbsp harissa paste or other chile paste
- ❏ The juice and zest of one orange
- ❏ 2 Tbsp salt
- ❏ 1 clove garlic, finely minced
- ❏ 1 tsp extra-virgin olive oil

Combine ingredients in a small bowl. Slather onto meat at least 30 minutes prior to smoking.

Paprika Herb Rub

Ingredients:
- ❏ 1 Tbsp paprika
- ❏ ½ tsp dried thyme
- ❏ ½ tsp dried rosemary
- ❏ ½ tsp dried oregano
- ❏ ½ tsp dried marjoram
- ❏ ½ tsp kosher salt
- ❏ ¼ tsp ground black pepper

Combine ingredients in a small bowl. Rub onto

meat and skin and allow to sit at least one hour before smoking. Unused portions can be kept in an airtight container for up to 6 months.

Rosemary Garlic Rub

This herby, garlicky wet rub is perfect for beef, lamb, and chicken.

Ingredients:
- ❏ 8 cloves garlic
- ❏ 3 Tbsp fresh rosemary
- ❏ 1 Tbsp kosher salt
- ❏ ⅓ cup olive oil

Pulse ingredients together in a food processor. Slather on the meat at least 30 minutes before smoking.

Salt and Pepper Steak Rub

Ingredients:
- ❏ 2 Tbsp coriander seeds, crushed
- ❏ 2 Tbsp cracked black pepper
- ❏ 2 tsp kosher salt
- ❏ 2 tsp dehydrated minced garlic
- ❏ 1 tsp crushed red pepper flake

Combine ingredients in a small bowl. Rub onto meat and skin and allow to sit at least one hour before smoking. Unused portions can be kept in an airtight container for up to 6 months.

Spicy Tunisian Rub

Ingredients:
- ❏ 2 tsp coriander seeds
- ❏ 2 tsp caraway seeds
- ❏ ¾ tsp crushed red pepper flake
- ❏ ¾ tsp garlic powder
- ❏ ½ tsp kosher salt

Combine ingredients in a spice grinder and grind until it forms a consistent powder. Rub onto meat and skin and allow to sit at least one hour before smoking. Unused portions can be kept in an airtight container for up to 6 months.

Sweet and Savory Dry Rub

Ingredients:
- ❏ 2 tsp light brown sugar
- ❏ 2 tsp dry mustard
- ❏ 1 tsp onion powder
- ❏ ½ tsp garlic powder
- ❏ ½ tsp salt
- ❏ ¼ tsp black pepper

Rub onto meat and skin and allow to sit at least one hour before smoking. Unused portions can be kept in an airtight container for up to 6 months.

Tuscan Spice Rub

Ingredients:
- ❏ 1 Tbsp fennel seeds
- ❏ 3 Tbsp dried basil
- ❏ 3 Tbsp garlic powder
- ❏ 2 Tbsp kosher salt
- ❏ 2 Tbsp dried rosemary
- ❏ 2 Tbsp dried oregano

Rub onto meat and skin and allow to sit at least one hour before smoking. Unused portions can be kept in an airtight container for up to 6 months.

MOPS & SAUCES

As is the case with all food, safety is the number one priority. If you are planning on serving sauce on the side of your cooked meat, remove a portion and set it aside prior to basting or mopping your meat. This will keep bacteria from the meat away from the sauce you serve to your guests.

Balsamic Barbecue Sauce

Ingredients:
- ❏ 1 cup balsamic vinegar
- ❏ ¾ cup ketchup
- ❏ ⅓ cup brown sugar
- ❏ 1 clove garlic, minced
- ❏ 1 Tbsp Worcestershire sauce
- ❏ 1 Tbsp Dijon mustard
- ❏ ½ tsp salt
- ❏ ½ tsp black pepper

In a small sauce pan, combine all ingredients and heat over low heat 15 to 20 minutes until sugar is dissolved and sauce is thickened. Brush over meat in the last 30 minutes of smoking to ensure it does not burn.

Barbecue Beef Mop

Ingredients:
- ❏ 2 cups beef stock
- ❏ 1 cup beer
- ❏ ⅓ cup Worcestershire sauce
- ❏ 1 ½ tsp salt
- ❏ 1 ½ tsp paprika
- ❏ 1 ½ tsp dry mustard
- ❏ 1 ½ tsp garlic powder
- ❏ 1 ½ tsp black pepper
- ❏ 1 ½ tsp cayenne

Combine all ingredients in a bowl or jar. Begin mopping beef midway through cooking and continue to mop each hour until the beef reaches the desired internal temperature. Discard unused mop.

Beer Mop for Brisket

Ingredients:
- ❏ 12 ounces dark beer
- ❏ ½ cup apple cider vinegar
- ❏ ⅓ cup water
- ❏ 1 small onion, diced
- ❏ 3 cloves garlic, minced
- ❏ 1 Tbsp Worcestershire sauce
- ❏ 1 Tbsp hot sauce
- ❏ 1 tsp black pepper

Combine all ingredients in a bowl or jar. Begin mopping beef midway through cooking and continue to mop each hour until the beef reaches the desired internal temperature. Discard unused mop.

Blueberry Barbecue Sauce

Ingredients:
- ❏ 1 14.5-ounce can diced tomatoes
- ❏ 2 cups blueberries
- ❏ 2 cloves garlic
- ❏ ¼ cup chopped yellow onion
- ❏ ¾ cup apple cider vinegar
- ❏ 2 Tbsp Worcestershire sauce
- ❏ ¼ cup light brown sugar
- ❏ 1 tsp Kosher salt
- ❏ 1 tsp ground black pepper
- ❏ ½ tsp ground coriander

Place ingredients into a blender and puree until smooth. Pour the sauce into a medium sized saucepan and bring to a simmer over medium heat. Cook, uncovered, until the volume reduces by 1/3, around 45 minutes.

Chinese Barbecue Sauce (Char Sui)

Ingredients:

- ❏ 2/3 cup hoisin sauce
- ❏ 2/3 cup soy sauce
- ❏ ½ cup sugar
- ❏ 4 cloves garlic, minced
- ❏ 2 tsp black bean paste
- ❏ 1 ½ tsp Chinese five spice powder
- ❏ 1 tsp salt

Combine all ingredients in a small sauce pan and heat over low, stirring constantly. Once mixture thickens, allow it to cool a few minutes before using.

Chipotle Mango Lime Barbecue Sauce

Ingredients:

- ❏ 1 mango, peeled, cored and cubed
- ❏ 2 cloves garlic
- ❏ 1 chipotle pepper in adobo sauce
- ❏ ½ cup ketchup
- ❏ The juice and zest of 1 lime
- ❏ 1 Tbsp melted butter
- ❏ 1 Tbsp brown sugar
- ❏ ½ tsp Kosher salt

Place all ingredients into a food processor and puree until smooth. Brush on chicken, pork or fish in the last 10-15 minutes of cooking.

Classic Texas Barbecue Sauce

Texas barbecue sauce is sweet, tangy, and just a little spicy. Since beef is the name of the game in Texas barbecue, this sauce can stand up to any brisket or burger but won't overpower pork or chicken.

Ingredients:

- ❏ 1 cup water
- ❏ 1 cup ketchup
- ❏ ½ cup apple cider vinegar
- ❏ ½ stick butter (¼ cup)
- ❏ ¼ cup minced onion

- ❏ ½ cup chopped celery
- ❏ 2 Tbsp Worcestershire sauce
- ❏ 2 Tbsp spicy mustard
- ❏ 2 Tbsp honey
- ❏ 2 cloves garlic, minced
- ❏ 1 beef bouillon cube or 1 Tbsp beef base
- ❏ 2 Tbsp chili powder
- ❏ ½ tsp salt
- ❏ ½ tsp pepper
- ❏ ¼ tsp cayenne pepper

Melt the butter in a medium-sized saucepan. Add onion and celery and cook until translucent. Add water and bouillon and stir until bouillon is dissolved. Add remaining ingredients and cook until the mixture has reduced by 1/3 and is thickened, around 15 minutes. Blend in a blender or food processor until smooth. Brush onto meat the last 15-30 minutes of cooking.

Cola Barbecue Sauce

This sweet, versatile sauce has a deep, rich color and satisfying tang. Substitute another soda (root beer, Dr. Pepper, or lemon lime soda) for a twist.

Ingredients:

- ❏ 2 Tbsp butter
- ❏ ½ cup onion, finely chopped
- ❏ 2 cups cola
- ❏ 2 cups ketchup
- ❏ ½ cup apple cider vinegar
- ❏ ¼ cup dark brown sugar
- ❏ 3 Tbsp chili powder
- ❏ 2 Tbsp paprika
- ❏ 1 Tbsp salt
- ❏ 2 tsp black pepper

Melt butter in a medium-sized saucepan over medium heat. Add onion and cook until soft and translucent, about 5 minutes. Add remaining ingredients and reduce heat to low. Simmer uncovered for 30-45 minutes or until the sauce thickens. For a smooth sauce, blend in a blender before using.

Coffee Spice Barbecue Sauce

This spicy, earthy sauce has a delightful bitter aftertaste from the coffee. It will remind you of mole, without the chocolate. Although a one ounce square of unsweetened chocolate would be delightful in this sauce...

Ingredients:

- ❏ 3 guajillo chiles
- ❏ 3 ancho chiles
- ❏ ½ cup onion, chopped
- ❏ 6 cloves garlic, whole
- ❏ 2 Tbsp vegetable oil
- ❏ 1 cup tomato puree
- ❏ 1 cup strong black coffee
- ❏ 2 tsp apple cider vinegar
- ❏ ¼ cup brown sugar
- ❏ 1 Tbsp salt
- ❏ 1 tsp dried oregano
- ❏ ¼ tsp cumin
- ❏ tsp cloves

Cut chiles in half and pull out seeds. Place in a large, dry skillet over medium high heat until fragrant, about 3 minutes. Turn for an additional minute. Put the chiles in a medium size bowl and cover with very hot water. Cover the bowl with plastic wrap and set aside for 30 minutes or until the chiles have softened. Drain the chiles, reserving the soaking liquid, and roughly chop the chiles. Set aside.

Meanwhile, place the onion and whole garlic cloves into the same dry skillet over medium heat until the onions char and the garlic softens. Cool.

Place the chiles and onion into a blender with as much of the soaking liquid needed to help the mixture break down into a paste. (About ¾ cup)

In the same skillet, heat the oil over medium-high heat. Add the chile mixture and cook until fragrant, about four minutes. Add the remaining ingredients except for the vinegar and stir. Reduce the heat to a simmer and cook until slightly thickened, about 15 minutes. Add the vinegar and adjust the seasonings according to taste.

Baste meat with the sauce during the last 30-60 minutes of cooking.

East Carolina Barbecue Sauce

Barbecue sauce in the eastern part of the Carolinas is made up of three basic items - apple cider vinegar, sugar, and crushed red pepper flake. Ours takes advantage of the garlicky flavor of Sriracha or sambal to kick the heat up a notch without sacrificing flavor. Unlike traditional thick barbecue sauces, this sauce is meant to be served on the table as the perfect complement to fatty pork dishes.

Ingredients:

- ❏ 2 cups apple cider vinegar
- ❏ 1 cup sugar
- ❏ ½ cup (one stick) butter
- ❏ 1 Tbsp Worcestershire
- ❏ 1 Tbsp ground dry mustard
- ❏ 1 Tbsp Sriracha or sambal
- ❏ 1 tsp crushed red pepper flake

In a medium saucepan, heat ingredients until sugar has dissolved. Cool and serve in a squeeze bottle alongside pulled pork.

Everything Basting Sauce

This sauce can be used for any recipe requiring a mop or basting sauce.

Ingredients:

- ❏ 1 quart apple cider vinegar
- ❏ 1 Tbsp garlic powder
- ❏ 1 Tbsp poultry seasoning
- ❏ 1 Tbsp crushed red pepper flake
- ❏ 1 Tbsp lemon pepper
- ❏ 1 tsp dried thyme
- ❏ 1 tsp dried rosemary
- ❏ 1 tsp salt
- ❏ 6 bay leaves

Heat ingredients over medium heat for 10 minutes to extract flavors from the herbs. Allow to cool before applying to the meat.

Frank's Buffalo Sauce

Taking a cue from buffalo wings, this sauce has a bit more complexity than the traditional buffalo sauce.

Ingredients:
- ❏ 1 cup Frank's red hot sauce
- ❏ ½ cup ketchup
- ❏ ¼ cup apple cider vinegar
- ❏ 2 Tbsp butter
- ❏ 2 tsp Worcestershire
- ❏ ¼ tsp celery seed

Combine ingredients in a small sauce pan over medium heat until thoroughly combined and heated through, around 5 minutes. Allow to cool before applying to meat.

Honey Chipotle Barbecue Sauce

Chipotle peppers in adobo sauce are a canned product available in the Latin foods aisle of the supermarket. This inexpensive ingredient packs a smoky, vinegary punch since chipotle peppers are actually dried, smoked jalapenos that have been canned in a thick vinegar sauce.

Ingredients:
- ❏ 1 cup finely diced onion
- ❏ 2 cloves garlic, minced
- ❏ 2 Tbsp extra-virgin olive oil
- ❏ 1 cup ketchup
- ❏ ¼ cup dark brown sugar
- ❏ ¼ cup honey
- ❏ 2 Tbsp apple cider vinegar
- ❏ 2 Tbsp molasses
- ❏ 3 chipotle peppers in adobo sauce, chopped
- ❏ 2 tsp Worcestershire sauce
- ❏ 2 tsp ancho chile powder
- ❏ 2 tsp smoked paprika
- ❏ 1 tsp cayenne pepper
- ❏ ½ tsp dry mustard

In a medium saucepan, heat olive oil over medium heat and saute onion and garlic for 3-5 minutes or until translucent. Add remaining ingredients and cook until thickened, around 10 minutes. Blend in a blender for a smooth sauce and allow to cool before applying to any meat.

Jeff Phillips' Mop Water

Jeff Phillips is one of the world's foremost barbecue aficionados. He uses this mop for his smoked brisket, but it would also be delicious on pork or chicken. You can easily purchase his specialty rubs and mops on his website.

Ingredients:
- ❏ 1 cup water
- ❏ 1 stick real butter
- ❏ 2 Tbsp prepared Cajun seasoning (Tony Cachere's is our favorite)

Heat ingredients together until butter is melted. Mop generously on the meat halfway through cooking.

Kansas City Barbecue Sauce

Traditional Kansas City barbecue sauce is sweet and thick with a touch of heat. This sauce does not disappoint and is perfect for ribs.

Ingredients:
- ❏ 1 ½ cup ketchup
- ❏ 1 cup water
- ❏ ❏ cup apple cider vinegar
- ❏ ¼ cup dark brown sugar
- ❏ 2 Tbsp molasses
- ❏ 1 Tbsp onion powder
- ❏ 1 Tbsp garlic powder
- ❏ 1 Tbsp black pepper
- ❏ 1 tsp celery salt
- ❏ 1 tsp allspice
- ❏ 1 tsp cayenne

Combine all ingredients in a small saucepan over medium heat until thoroughly combined. Reduce heat to a simmer until thickened, around 10 minutes. Allow to cool before applying to meat. Brush meat with the sauce the last 15-30 minutes of cooking to prevent it from burning.

> **Tip:** Allspice is actually not a combination of spices as the name suggests. Even though it tastes like a combination of cinnamon, nutmeg, and clove, it is the berry from the allspice bush.

- ❏ 2 tsp black pepper
- ❏ 1 tsp dried thyme

Combine ingredients in a small saucepan over medium heat for 10 minutes to allow flavors to combine. Cool before applying to meat halfway through smoking.

Memphis Barbecue Sauce

While Memphis barbecue is all about the dry rub, if you insist on sauce on your Memphis barbecue, this is the one. Pitmaster Meathead Goldwyn claims this recipe actually requires two cups of bourbon - one and a half cups for the sauce and a half cup for the sauce maker.

Ingredients:
- ❏ 1 ½ cup bourbon
- ❏ 1 cup ketchup
- ❏ 1 Tsp lemon juice
- ❏ 2 Tbsp Worcestershire sauce
- ❏ 2 Tbsp apple cider vinegar
- ❏ ¼ cup molasses

In a small saucepan over medium heat, pour in 1 cup bourbon. Allow the bourbon to reduce to around 2 Tbsp Add the remaining ingredients including the last ½ cup bourbon. Allow to simmer another 30 minutes or until the sauce has reduced by ⅔. Use immediately or reserve it in the jar for up to one month.

Memphis Mop

Lightly applying this mop during smoking will keep ribs moist and tender.

Ingredients:
- ❏ 1 cup water
- ❏ ½ cup apple cider vinegar
- ❏ 3 Tbsp paprika
- ❏ 2 Tbsp dry mustard
- ❏ 1 Tbsp onion powder
- ❏ 1 Tbsp garlic powder
- ❏ 1 Tbsp crushed red pepper flake

Peach Mustard Barbecue Sauce

If you're tired of tomato based barbecue sauces, this sweet and tangy sauce is the perfect out-of-the-ordinary barbecue sauce for chicken, fish, or pork.

Ingredients:
- ❏ 4 Tbsp butter (½ stick)
- ❏ ¼ cup minced onion
- ❏ 3 cloves, minced
- ❏ ¼ cup apple cider vinegar
- ❏ ½ cup whole grain mustard
- ❏ ¼ cup Dijon mustard
- ❏ 1 cup peach jam or preserves
- ❏ ½ tsp salt

In a medium saucepan over medium heat, melt butter until foamy. Add onion and garlic and cook until translucent. Add remaining ingredients and simmer for 10 minutes until thick. For a smoother sauce, puree in a food processor or blender. Brush sauce on chicken, pork, or fish during the last 15-30 minutes of cooking.

Peanut Sauce

Not only does this sauce make a fantastic barbecue sauce on chicken, it is also a phenomenal dipping sauce for egg rolls or chicken wings.

Ingredients:
- ❏ 4 tsp toasted sesame oil
- ❏ 3 Tbsp fresh lime juice
- ❏ 2 Tbsp soy sauce
- ❏ 2 tsp Asian hot chili sauce or Sriracha
- ❏ 2 garlic cloves, minced
- ❏ 2 green onions, finely chopped
- ❏ 1 cup sweet pepper relish

- ❏ 1 Tbsp ginger, freshly grated
- ❏ ½ cup cocktail peanuts, finely chopped

Combine all ingredients in a bowl and allow to sit at least 30 minutes before using.

Quick Barbecue Sauce

If ketchup based sauces are too sweet, using whole tomatoes will take the edge off of the sweetness and allow you to control how much sugar is in your sauce.

Ingredients:
- ❏ 2 Tbsp extra-virgin olive oil
- ❏ 1 cup chopped onion
- ❏ 6 cloves garlic, minced
- ❏ 1 Tbsp tomato paste
- ❏ 1 can whole, peeled tomatoes (with puree), pureed in a blender
- ❏ 1 cup apple cider vinegar
- ❏ 1 cup firmly packed light brown sugar
- ❏ 1½ tsp salt
- ❏ Freshly ground black pepper

In a medium saucepan, heat oil over medium heat. Saute onion and garlic until soft and translucent. Add tomato paste and cook until the tomato paste turns brick red. Add pureed tomatoes, vinegar, brown sugar, salt and pepper and simmer over low heat until thickened, about 30 minutes. Allow to cool before applying to meat.

Southern Barbecue Sauce

The Carolinas are known for vinegar based sauces. But travel a few hundred miles south and you'll find a ketchup-based sauce that is tangy, less sweet than Kansas City style sauce, and spicier than Texas barbecue sauce.

Ingredients:
- ❏ 1 ½ cups ketchup
- ❏ ⅔ cup apple cider vinegar
- ❏ ½ cup water
- ❏ ¼ cup butter (½ stick)
- ❏ 2 Tbsp Worcestershire Sauce

- ❏ 2 Tbsp brown sugar
- ❏ 1 tsp paprika
- ❏ 1 tsp garlic powder
- ❏ 1 tsp hot sauce
- ❏ ¼ tsp cayenne pepper
- ❏ The juice of one lemon

Combine all ingredients except for lemon juice in a medium saucepan over low heat. Simmer for 30 minutes until sauce thickens slightly. Remove from heat and stir in lemon juice. Allow to cool before applying to meat.

St. Louis Barbecue Sauce

St. Louis barbecue sauce is a thinner, tangier version of its Kansas City cousin.

Ingredients:
- ❏ 2 cups ketchup
- ❏ ½ cup water
- ❏ ⅔ cup apple cider vinegar
- ❏ ⅔ cup brown sugar
- ❏ 2 Tbsp yellow mustard
- ❏ 1 Tbsp onion powder
- ❏ 1 Tbsp garlic powder
- ❏ ½ tsp cayenne pepper
- ❏ ¼ tsp salt

Combine ingredients in a bowl. Allow to sit for at least 30 minutes before using.

Sweet and Sour Barbecue Sauce

This Asian-inspired sauce is a great addition to spare ribs that have been rubbed with our Asian rub.

Ingredients:
- ❏ 1 Tbsp extra-virgin olive oil
- ❏ 2 cloves garlic, chopped
- ❏ 2 Tbsp finely grated peeled fresh ginger
- ❏ ½ c dry sherry
- ❏ ½ cup hoisin sauce
- ❏ ½ cup ketchup
- ❏ ¼ cup rice wine vinegar
- ❏ 2 Tbsp sugar

- ❏ 2 tsp sambal or Sriracha
- ❏ 2 tsp soy sauce
- ❏ 2 tsp sesame oil

In a saucepan, heat olive oil. Add garlic and ginger and cook until fragrant. Add remaining ingredients and simmer over low heat for 10 minutes. Allow to cool before applying to meat.

Texas Hillbilly Mop Sauce

Because this mop doesn't have any sugar, you can easily use it as a marinade since it won't burn.

Ingredients:
- ❏ 2 cups apple cider vinegar
- ❏ ⅓ cup Worcestershire sauce
- ❏ ½ cup water
- ❏ 2 sticks melted butter
- ❏ ½ cup lemon juice
- ❏ 2 Tbsp hot sauce
- ❏ 6 bay leaves, crushed
- ❏ 2 cloves garlic, minced
- ❏ 1 Tbsp paprika
- ❏ 1 Tbsp chili powder

Heat all ingredients together in a medium saucepan for 10 minutes to combine flavors. Allow to cool before marinating or mopping meat.

White Barbecue Sauce

White barbecue sauce is ideal for poultry. Marinate your birds in it for tender, flavorful meat or brush it on during the last 30 minutes of cooking.

Ingredients:
- ❏ 1 cup mayonnaise
- ❏ ½ cup apple cider vinegar
- ❏ ¼ cup lemon juice
- ❏ ¼ cup apple juice
- ❏ 2 Tbsp horseradish
- ❏ 1 Tbsp garlic powder
- ❏ 1 Tbsp onion powder
- ❏ 1 Tbsp ground black pepper
- ❏ 1 tsp dry mustard powder
- ❏ ½ tsp salt
- ❏ ½ tsp cayenne pepper

Combine all ingredients in a medium bowl. Cover and chill at least one hour before using.

TOOLS OF THE TRADE

Aside from your Masterbuilt® smoker, there are a few helpful tools that will make your barbecue experience easier.

Tool	What It Is Used For	Approximate Cost
Meat Thermometer	Checking your meat for doneness. Remember, cook to temperature, not to time. If your Masterbuilt® Smoker is not equipped with a digital meat thermometer, this is the next tool to buy.	Varies according to features. $5-$150
Turkey Fryer	Three words. Smo-fried turkey.	$80-$200
Carving Gloves	These heat-proof gloves are perfect for handling briskets, pulling pork, or moving meat into or out of the smoker.	$5-$20
Chef's Knife	Just because you never EVER check the doneness of your meat by cutting into it, doesn't mean you won't need a knife for carving it after it is finished. Look for a knife that is comfortable in your hand.	A good quality knife can be found in the $30-$50 range.
Filet Knife	Ideal for butterflying meat you intend to stuff and tie.	A good quality knife can be found in the $30-$50 range.
Small saucepot	Simmering mop sauce or glazing sauces for application. Look for a pot that can be used over a gas fire.	$20-30

Getting Started With Your Masterbuilt®

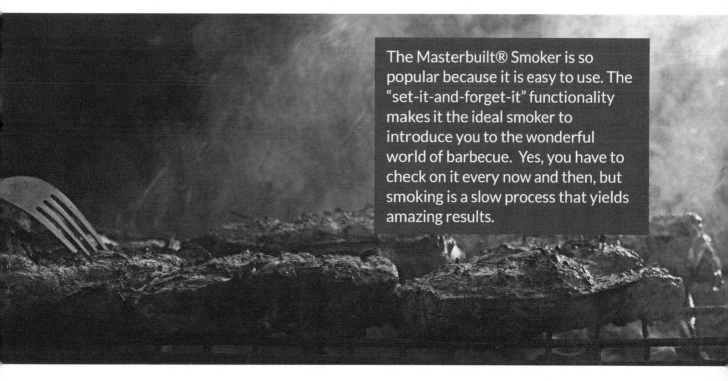

The Masterbuilt® Smoker is so popular because it is easy to use. The "set-it-and-forget-it" functionality makes it the ideal smoker to introduce you to the wonderful world of barbecue. Yes, you have to check on it every now and then, but smoking is a slow process that yields amazing results.

Did you just open your new Masterbuilt® Smoker?

Be sure to follow the instructions on pre-seasoning your new smoker before using it to cook food. When these machines are shipped from the factory, they are covered in metallic dust and industrial chemicals that could end up in your food. These mysterious additives do not make great barbecue.

1. The secret to great tasting barbecue is cooking meat low and slow. The Masterbuilt® will do most of the work for you since it's largely designed to be a "set-it-and-forget-it" machine, but you must plan ahead if you want everything to go smoothly. Be prepared to do a lot of waiting -- but it will absolutely be worth it!

2. The secret to cooking multiple pieces of meat is to know exactly when to put in and take out each type of meat. The key is to pay attention to the different smoke times of every piece of meat going in the smoker. For example, if you're smoking six Cornish hens, they all have the same smoke time, so they come out at the same time. But if you're cooking a pork butt, chicken wings, and ribs, you have to make a plan for the time each meat spends in the smoker. The estimated cooking time is included with each recipe, so as long as you set a timer and mind your thermometer, everything will come out perfectly.

Sample Plan For Cooking Multiple Pieces of Meat

Type of Meat	Size/Weight	Required Time	Start Time	Finish Time
Pork Butt	8 lbs	13 hours	5:00 AM	6:00 PM
Ribs	1 Rack	6 hours	12:00 PM	6:00 PM
Chicken Wings	3 lbs	2 hours	4:00 PM	6:00 PM

3. When cooking outside in cold temperatures, expect to increase your cooking time.

4. Technical details.
   - Max temperature of the smoker is 275°F
   - Your Masterbuilt® Smoker is equipped with a water pan. This allows your smoker to generate steam as well as smoke to help in temperature regulation. In cold temperatures, the water pan will maintain heat inside of your smoker. In warmer temperatures, it will prevent the smoker from getting too hot. The water pan also gives you an opportunity to infuse more flavor into your product by adding herbs or whole spices to the water. The only time you do NOT want to add water to the pan is during the seasoning process.

Do:

1. Use ½ cup of woodchips at a time to generate thick smoke. Wood pellets and chunks are not recommended for use in the woodchip tray.
2. Preheat the smoker for 30-40 minutes at max temperature before loading food.
3. Check the grease tray often during cooking and empty it before it gets too full.
4. Store your smoker in a dry area when not in use.
5. Keep the smoker door closed when adding wood chips. Every time the door is opened, heat is lost and cooking time increases.

Don't:

1. Don't run the smoker in closed places like garages. This is an outdoor smoker, smoking indoors is very dangerous.
2. Don't open the smoker door unless you really have to.
3. Don't start the smoker without the wood chip loader and tray in place. Otherwise, you could get wood flare-ups.
4. Don't let the smoker sit on uneven surfaces that could cause it to tip. That's just a bad idea.
5. Don't use an extension cord
6. Don't cover the metal racks with aluminum foil. This prevents air from circulating through the smoker and can cause uneven heating, and sometimes severe damage.

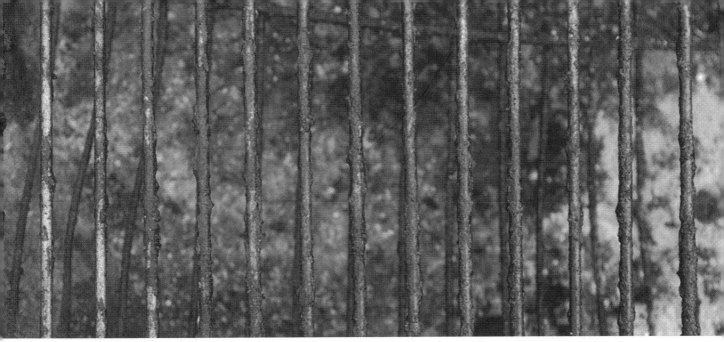

Cleaning your smoker:

1. The metal grates, water bowl and drip pan should all be cleaned using a mild soap solution. Rinse and dry completely.
2. The smoke build-up in the machine will likely cause the interior walls to blacken with residue. Thoroughly wipe down both the interior and exterior with a damp cloth. Do not use chemical cleaning agents as this could potentially damage the electric smoker or cause a fire.
3. The inside seam where the door seal attaches to the door should be wiped down with a damp cloth after each use. This is important to keep both the door and inner seam functioning properly -- otherwise, smoke could start leaking out.
4. The woodchip tray and loader fill up with ash, smoke residue and dust frequently. Masterbuilt® recommends disposing of the cold ashes by brushing them into aluminum foil, soaking it with water to prevent flare-ups. Throw the discarded ash wrapped in foil in a non-combustible container.

After each use, be sure to:
1. Clean out old ashes piling up in the woodchip tray.
2. Clean out grease tray.
3. Wipe down the inside of the smoker with a damp cloth -- including the door seal and the inside seam that the door seal attaches to.
4. Wipe the meat probe clean.

Using Your Masterbuilt®

Using the Digital Controls

To set temperature:
1. Press on button.
2. Press SET TEMP button after LED display blinks to life.
3. Use the "+/-" to set temperature.
4. Press SET TEMP again to finalize temperature selection.

To set timer:
1. Press SET TIME button after LED display for hours blinks
2. Use the "+/-" to set time.
3. Press SET TIME button again to lock in time was selected. Next the minutes section will start blinking
4. Use the "+/-" to set temperature.
5. Press SET TIME to lock in minutes and start the cooking cycle.

Using the Meat Probe:

1. Insert meat probe right into the center of meat to get an accurate reading.
2. Press and hold MEAT PROBE button, and the LED display will reveal the internal temperature of the meat being probed.
3. Once MEAT PROBE button is released-LED display will return to set temperature or set time.

To use light:
1. Press LIGHT button to switch light on.
2. Press LIGHT button to switch light off.
3. To RESET control panel:
4. If control panel shows an error message, turn electric smoker off, unplug unit from outlet, wait ten seconds, plug unit back into outlet, then turn electric smoker on. This will reset control panel.

Using the Air Damper

The air damper is designed to steadily release moisture from the smoker as food cooks inside. Depending on the model of the Masterbuilt® you have, you might find it either on the side, back or the top of the smoker.

It is generally recommended that you close the air damper anywhere from ¾ to ½ open for most foods, as this will allow the moisture building up inside to escape through the air damper slowly. Moisture is important in the cooking process to create juicy, tender meat. When cooking dried foods such as jerky, however, you want to open the air damper even more to allow the meat to dry out completely.

Using the Woodchip Tray

1. Preheat the smoker before adding wood chips or setting meat inside the machine.
2. After the desired temperature has been reached, place the water bowl filled with water in the bottom of the smoker (optional)
3. Fill the woodchip tray with a small handful of woodchips and push it back into its slot, then twist to dump the wood chips into the heating element inside..
4. Let it burn for about two hours, and add wood chips again as needed during the smoking process.
5. Feel free to use various types of wood chips to get different smoky flavors: hickory, apple, pecan, and mesquite are quite popular.

Using the Remote:

Some Masterbuilt® smokers come equipped with a digital remote control that offers truly hands-off barbecuing. To use your remote control:
1. Press the ON button.
2. Press SET TEMP button once. The LED display will flash.
3. Use +/- to set the desired temperature.
4. Press SET TEMP button to lock in the temperature.

Note: Heating will not begin until timer is set. To set the timer:

1. Press SET TIME button once. The LED display for hours will flash.
2. Use +/- to set hours.
3. Press SET TIME button again to lock in the hours timer.
4. The minutes LED will flash.
5. Use +/- to set minutes.
6. Press SET TIME button again to lock in the minutes and start the cook cycle.

The heat will automatically turn off when time has expired.

To replace the remote batteries:
- Slide the belt clip to the left to remove.
- Press tab down on battery cover and pull out.
- Install 2 "AAA" Alkaline batteries.
- Replace the battery cover.
- Remove the batteries before storing remote control.

How to Preseason Your New Smoker:

1. Clean the inside of the smoker with mild soap and water. Be sure to wipe every inch of the inside down. Rinse everything down with water and let air-dry.
2. Spray the inside with cooking oil, coating all surfaces. Be sure not to over-spray so that oil is dripping off the sides, just enough to coat the surface.
3. Place the empty water pan inside and set the smoker to smoke for 3 hours on max temp.

General cooking tips:

1. Sometimes the meat reaches the desired temperature before you're ready to serve. If this case, wrap it in aluminum foil and reduce the temperature until it is time to eat.
2. Do not overload the smoker. This extends cooking time and may cause food to cook unevenly since heat is not allowed to circulate throughout the smoker.
3. If you want to apply barbecue sauce or other wet ingredients, apply the sauce to the meat an hour before it is finished cooking and then wrap with foil.
4. Dry rubs are okay to apply to the meat before placing in the smoker.
5. Do not cover the racks with aluminum foil since this will prevent heat from circulating inside effectively.

Masterbuilt® Accessories

Racks & Grates:

1. Masterbuilt® rib rack
   A metal rack specifically designed to hold up to six slabs of rib meat. You will have to remove a smoker grate or two to get the rib rack to fit inside.
2. Regular smoker grate
   This is the standard smoker grate that comes with the MES®. If the grates that came with the MES® are lost, damaged or just deteriorating in quality, you can easily replace them by purchasing more smoker grates.
3. Sausage hanger
   The sausage hanger is perfect for curing and smoking your own homemade sausages with the electric smoker. Several smoker grates have to be removed to be able to use this add-on.

Smoker Add-ons:

1. Masterbuilt® cold smoking kit
   This add-on is the official attachment that was specifically designed for the MES®. The stock woodchip feeder that comes with the MES® has to be cleaned and refilled every 30 minutes or so -- who has the time to babysit? This cold smoking kit has dual purposes: (1) you can run it with the MES® on for extended smoking without having to constantly refill woodchips, or (2) you can turn the MES® off and run the cold smoker at temperatures as low as 100⬚ to cold smoke your food.

2. Electric smoker cover
   A durable weather-resistant cover is a no-brainer for protecting your MES® from harsh weather conditions.

3. Smoker side shelf
   This is a great add-on, but not necessary if you have a cooking space set up outside. Add this to your smoker if you want a nice side shelf for storing spices or tools. Do a little research first, because this shelf was not designed to work with every MES® model.

4. Electric smoker stand
   This stand is great if you want to raise your smoker 16 inches above the ground for easier access. They are currently only built for the 30" MES® models, but this might change later on. Check on Amazon to be sure your model will work with this stand.

Unofficial add-ons:

Unofficial add-ons are not sanctioned by the Masterbuilt® company, so use these at your own risk. However, many people claim to have a lot of success with the following products.

1. A-MAZE-N-PELLET-SMOKER 5x8 (https://www.amazenproducts.com) Similar to the Masterbuilt® Cold Smoking Kit, this simple add-on is essentially a tray that can withstand high heat and is placed inside the bottom of the smoker while cooking. It is filled with up to 1 lb. of pellets -- which are not recommended for the Masterbuilt®'s stock woodchip tray -- and provides continuous thick smoke for 8-10 hours.

Masterbuilt® Reviews

We combed through hundreds of reviews online and compiled a condensed list of things that people either love or hate about the Masterbuilt® Smoker.

Things People Love:

- The handheld remote control is a super convenient feature. It will allow you to program the time and temperature and check the meat probe temperature.
- Solid construction. The machine is well-built and the material used is high quality.
- Great for cooking for lots of people as there is a lot of room inside.
- Ease of use. Because this machine is digital, it is very easy to monitor and check up on. Great for beginners or advanced barbecue aficionados.
- Very economical. It runs on electricity and with small amounts of wood, relatively speaking. You can save a lot of money in the long run if you smoke a lot of meat.

Common Complaints:

- Barbecue purists say you're losing something by not burning a real wood or charcoal fire. This smoker does not replace a high heat grill like a gas grill. (But you can always finish off the smoked meat in a gas grill if you have one)
- Many people complain about the smoke tray not working correctly no matter what they tried. (This can be solved by requesting a retrofit kit from Masterbuilt®, which they should send for free if you are in the warranty period)
- Several people have been complaining that their machine stop working after only a few uses. (However, their customer service seems quite responsive and willing to help you solve all issues)
- The heat retention is a common problem. But this issue exists for virtually every smoker or grill on the market. Opening the door for even a few seconds can cause the internal temperature to drop by 50° or more immediately.
- Over time, the machine can develop a metallic smell that affects the smoke. Some people report that this machine gives a smoky/metallic odor.

A Message From Big Bob

Barbecue is as much a state of mind as it is a way to prepare food. It cannot be rushed. There are no shortcuts. It is a creative outlet for all of your wildest food dreams, but at the root of it all, there is fire and smoke.

Imagine if you will, a cool spring morning. The world is quiet except for the chirping birds in the trees. As you load a dry rubbed pork butt into your smoker, you marvel at the glorious sunrise over the horizon and the smell of wood smoke meeting your nostrils. In that brief moment, all is right with the world.

Hours later you return to reload the smoker with wood chips, cold beverage in one hand, warm afternoon sun on your shoulders. You begin thinking about how to garnish your masterpiece - sauce, salad, bread, vegetables.

Finally, the moment of truth arrives. Opening the door you are met with a symphony of aromas. Smoke, pork, and the sweet and spicy rub all greet you like old friends and it is all you can do to not lift the five pound piece of other-worldly deliciousness directly to your lips.

Barbecue connects us to our most primal ancestors. Cowboys on the open range, pioneers taming an untamable land, hunters and gatherers in the mountains of a far distant country all had one thing in common. Meat met fire and they were the master of it all. But more importantly, this process brought families and communities together.

In the 1800s, families would come together to slaughter pigs in the fall. Every part was used and every family member had a job. Ham and bacon would be salted and smoked. Pieces and parts would be cooked with herbs and the meat ground into sausage. Fat would be rendered and skin fried into cracklins. Every part was used and what resulted was a family that could eat well through the winter.

Fast forward 200 years and today's pitmasters travel from town to town, setting up enormous smokers and honing their craft in competition. At the heart of the silly hats and insanely delicious food is a sense of community that has all but disappeared from our modern lives.

Today's modern smokers have made barbecue more readily available to the amateur, giving new cooks the ability to experiment with flavor combinations without the worry over temperature maintenance so common with traditional smokers. While there are a few basic rules for cuts of meat, temperature, and cooking time, barbecue is open to your interpretation. But most importantly, it is meant to bring your family, friends, and community together.

Next time you are at the market, pick up that extra large pork shoulder and invite the neighbors over. You will not only be the master of fire and smoke, but also the hero of your neighborhood.

Barbecue Basics In A Nutshell

Ask any barbecue world champion how to create amazing barbecue and they will tell you the same thing -- it's hard work. Your food is never going to come out right if you don't respect the fact that there is a tested method to making meat taste phenomenal.

But most of us don't invest hundreds or thousands of dollars in smokers and other cooking equipment to start competing against serious professionals who devote their lives to this art. What we want is to understand the smoking process thoroughly, so that we can consistently create spectacular-tasting meat that draws crowds and impresses our party guests.

This book draws knowledge from tons of serious resources -- highly-rated barbecue books, professional barbecue experts, meat science research papers, and meat smoking forums. What you are getting is the best of the best information, diluted down to a simple step-by-step process that anyone can follow.

But the *most important* thing that everyone seems to forget when they start learning the basics is that this is supposed to be fun. Don't kill yourself over cooking times and temperatures if you want to cook like a trained professional. These experts have spent thousands of hours cooking the same dishes over and over, changing only one or two things at a time to test whether those small changes resulted in better tasting food.

Rather than letting you become a slave to recipes and procedures, this book will force you to use your senses while cooking and learn how to make exceptional barbecue just by looking, smelling, touching, and tasting. You will learn to ask yourself:

Is the inside of this brisket the right color?

Are these spareribs moist and tender enough?

Will this homemade spice rub come out right?

What should amazing barbecue taste like?

Ah, the infamous question that keeps meat enthusiasts up at night. The shocking answer is that everyone's tastes are different, so amazing barbecue should taste like *what you think makes it great*.

Okay, that answer was a bit of a cop-out. But it's true. Just because one expert tells you that the best damned ribs must be seasoned and cooked this way or that way doesn't mean you have to follow every step , er, to the bone. Instead, focus on learning the techniques and bend what you learn to suit your tastebuds.

That being said, there are a few universal qualities to amazing barbecue:

1. **The essence is in the meat.** The natural flavor of the cut of meat you cook should always come through. There are so many animal parts to choose from, each with their own personalities. And not all animals will taste the same consistently -- everything from how the animal was born, raised and butchered to how that animal's meat was transported, stored and prepared can affect the end result.

2. **The secondary flavors.** There are millions of spice rubs, brines, marinades, mops, and sauces that you could use to flavor your meat. Great barbecue should have layers of flavor that complement each other and are well-balanced. The most important layer will always be the natural flavor of the meat, but the secondary flavors are even more subjective because everyone has their own preferences about what kind of barbecue they like -- spicy, sweet, bitter, salty or sour. The secondary layers are where you have total control over the final taste of the barbecue since you can't do much to change the taste of the meat besides buying from high-quality sources.

3. **The texture.** The third most universally revered quality about barbecue is that it should essentially be moist and tender. There are people who literally drive

hundreds and hundreds of miles, often across state lines, just to experience the sensation of biting into super juicy, tender meat.

4. **The flavor of the smoke.** The final quality that makes for essential barbecue is the flavor of the smoke that penetrates the meat. Smoke is celebrated by carnivores everywhere for its ability to deepen the flavor of meat and soften its chewy texture. It is what brings together all the other qualities discussed above through the "low and slow" indirect cooking process. This is why smoking meat takes much longer than grilling, because we are indirectly cooking the food, rather than directly over a fire.

What is the difference between grilling and barbecuing?

Cooking food with smoke is a time-consuming process, and that is why it is inherently different from grilling. Rather than cooking food fast over high heat (350-400°F and up), smoking requires cooking the food slowly in low, indirect heat (350°F and lower), and needs lots of smoke.

Grilling is perfect for meat that is already tender, and, of course, searing the outside to create a wonderful crispy texture. But when you barbecue, you are cooking meat while infusing it with the flavors of smoke and tenderizing it at the same time. Here is a general rule to remember -- pretty much anything you grill can be barbecued, but not everything that is barbecued can be grilled.

A Quick Breakdown Of What Meat Is Made Of

Depending on the animal you're looking at, most lean muscle tissue is generally 75% water, 20% protein, 5% fat, sugars, minerals and vitamins. Of course, different cuts will vary in these numbers, but it is important to have an overview of what meat is made of to be able to control the cooking process.

When an animal grazes a field, takes long walks, runs away from threats, and all the other wonderful things animals do, its muscles get tougher and need more oxygen. A compound called myoglobin accepts fuel from blood in the form of oxygen and iron, so the more active an animal is, the more myoglobin it needs. Myoglobin is what causes meat to turn darker and more flavorful.

White meat, like the kind in chicken breasts, is only meant for fast bursts of explosive energy -- not extended periods of exercise. This is why the lower part of the chicken tends to be darker, since the legs are constantly walking. Birds like ducks or geese tend to be dark all around because all their muscles are actively being used when walking, flying or swimming.

The Science of Cooking Meat

Understanding the magic behind cooking irresistible barbecue is really just learning a little science. When heat is applied to meat, it starts breaking down physically and chemically -- a process known as denaturing. If you learn how to control how the meat changes, you will master the process of creating flavorful and tender meat over and over again.

White meat vs. dark meat

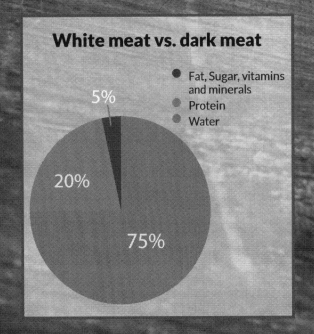

- Fat, Sugar, vitamins and minerals
- Protein
- Water

5%
20%
75%

Muscle fibers

Muscle fibers are basically tubes of fiber that are called sheaths when bundled together. A whole bunch of sheaths bundled together are what make up the muscle. These fibers are like threads filled with water and different kinds of proteins -- actin and myosin being the most important since they control the muscle's basic movements by either letting it contract or relax. When an animal grows as nature intended, its muscle fibers get bigger and tougher from exercise.

Connective tissue

Without connective tissue, the meat would just fall off the bone -- and no, not in the delicious barbecue way. Most people are familiar with tendons, which directly keep the muscles attached to the bone, but the shiny thin wrapping you see around muscles known as silverskin is also a type of connective tissue that is keeping different kinds of muscles attached together.

Collagen is a soft connective tissue that is found throughout the muscle, usually near fibers and sheaths by holding them together. This tissue melts into a liquid when heated, and covers the muscles in a silky coating that can also add moisture. Melting collagen takes time, so that's why tough cuts of meat are cooked low and slow over a long period of time.

Fats are a type of lipid that give the muscles energy. They can be found beneath the skin, between layers of muscle groups and even stitched inside the muscle fibers and sheaths. Fat is very important in the cooking process because it is absolutely delicious and absorbs much of the essential flavors of the food the animal consumes. Marbling is typically intramuscular fat, and can be seen as thin white or yellow lines in the surface of the meat.

Water content in meat is unfortunately underrated. Most of the liquid in meat is water! No, that red juice leaking out of your meat is not blood (blood is much darker and thicker). The water in the meat is important because it is the most basic source of nutrition for every living thing. We tend to take water quality for granted, but don't forget that everything the animal eats or drinks ends up in its muscles, and eventually in yours if you eat it.

THE SCIENCE OF FLAVOR

According to science, flavor is made up of three basic things:
1. Taste
2. Physical stimulation
3. Smell

We have tiny receptors in our taste buds that bind to specific compounds that tell us whether what we're eating is sweet, salty, bitter, or sour -- the four basic tastes. But our tongues can taste more than just these four sensations by combining hundreds of compounds, all of which go through chemical and physical changes when cooked.

Physical stimulation comprises of all the physical qualities of biting, chewing and swallowing food. When you chomp on a chicken wing, you experience layers of different textures -- crispy skin, juicy meat and a hard bone in the center. Even the sounds of biting into different foods affect the physical experience, just as their appearance would. When you eat spicy habanero wings, the burning sensation and pain in your mouth is also considered physical stimulation.

Smell is a complicated sense because it is so closely related to taste. It is believed that most of the flavor that comes from smoke is smell. Smoke consists of water vapor, gases and the tiny particles that result from combusting wood (cellulose and lignin, if you're curious). Smell is probably the most important sense because it is a very powerful stimulus, capable of triggering vivid personal memories unlike any other sense in our body.

FAQ

What is smoke?

Smoke is a complicated byproduct of combusting natural elements such as wood, charcoal or gas. It contains lots of microscopic compounds like creosote, ash, carbon dioxide, carbon monoxide, water vapor, and phenols to name a few. Depending on what you're combusting, the list of contents in the smoke will vary. If you cooked a pair of spare ribs with the same rub on two different grills -- one over a gas grill and the other over charcoal, you can actually see and taste the difference. They both will taste fantastic, but noticeably different. This is why some barbecue aficionados buy more than one kind of smoker.

What kind of smoke should I be looking for?

The nature of smoke depends on several factors ranging from the source of heat to the setup of the smoker. The type of smoke coveted by experts is thin blue smoke; it won't actually be deep blue, but a bluish gray tint. The color is determined by the amount of particles present in the smoke and how well those particles are spreading out.

Black and gray smoke is a result of the fire being deprived of oxygen -- it can make your food taste bitter and nasty, kind of like an ashtray. Billowing white smoke appears as a thick cloud and is also not the kind of smoke you want to cook with. The best way to achieve thin blue smoke is to use natural wood as a heat source, keep the smoker clean of sticky grease and creosote and finally, make sure the fire is getting oxygen.

Why does poultry and pork sometimes stay pink inside when fully cooked?

The simple answer to this question is carbon monoxide, a gas that reacts with myoglobin in meat and turns it pink. Grilling or smoking with heat sources such as charcoal, wood or gas produce plenty of carbon monoxide. Some other causes could be presence of nitrites in the meat or in leafy vegetables that transfer to the meat during the cooking process.

This is why using a thermometer is always highly recommended. Checking for doneness can be deceiving because judging the meat just by its color is simply not reliable.

Should I soak my wood?

Many people think soaking wood enhances the flavor of their meat, but wet wood doesn't produce desirable smoke. It also increases the cooking time by as much as 20-30 minutes because it cools the fire. The best kind of smoke is very thin and pale blue, a quality which can only be achieved by using dry wood.

What are smoke rings?

The pink layer directly below the bark is referred to as the smoke ring. This coveted ring is one of the things people look for when they pull their meat out of the smoker and cut the meat open. If the smoke ring is there, they believe that the meat "has arrived" and the smoking process went exactly as it was supposed to.

Instead, what is actually happening is that gases such as carbon monoxide and nitrogen monoxide are reacting with the iron in myoglobin present just below the surface of the meat. These gases are not able to penetrate very far beyond the surface, so that is why the "smoke ring" is never found in the center of the meat. Many meat packers already inject their meat with carbon monoxide to keep the meat looking nice and pink. So basically, you really don't even need smoke to get that pink color.

What is "bark" and how do I get it on my meat?

The bark is the dark-colored crust that forms around meat that many people go nuts over because it is rich in flavor and very satisfying to chew. It's basically almost burnt and can range from a deep amber to dark browns. If it looks black, however, that means it was overcooked and is not good for you.

The tasty bark forms as a result of a chemical reaction between the spice rub coating the surface and the proteins in the meat fusing together. Fats from within the meat bubble up and mix with the rub also. Smoke gets absorbed in this sticky substance as its forming around the surface, turning it into delicious "meat candy."

If you're craving more bark, consider cutting the meat in half to expose more surface area for you to coat with dry rub.

What is juiciness and how do I help my meat stay juicy?

Meat is made up of around 75% water. Not blood, water. But what cooks refer to as "juiciness" goes beyond the water content in the finished product.

Scientists have been able to measure tenderness with the amount of pressure it takes to cut a piece of meat, however juiciness can only be measured by human experience. In reality, a piece of pork shoulder that has been cooked way past "well done", reaching an internal temperature of 200°, is considered "juicy" where a piece of steak cooked to an internal temperature of 200° is considered inedible charcoal. The difference? Fat and connective tissue.

In order for a piece of meat to retain its juiciness, it must be cooked the appropriate length of time in order to reach the appropriate internal temperature for that cut of meat. Like we've said before, temperature matters more than time and the cut you are using matters almost as much as temperature. Later in this guide you will find a comprehensive meat buying guide to help you choose the appropriate cut of meat for your smoker.

That being said, beginner barbecuers tend to have a better barbecue experience when they choose a less expensive cut of meat with a lot of fat and connective tissue. These pieces are more forgiving of the "low and slow" process, only getting better the longer they are cooked. As the fat and connective tissue melt, they become juicier and more succulent than their leaner counterparts, yielding a delicious end product.

What is "The Stall Zone" and how do I get past it?

When cooking large piece of meat such as a pork shoulder or brisket, the internal temperature will rise quickly over the first two or three hours and then stop going up. This is called "The Stall Zone" and has been making beginner barbecuers panic for generations. Despite speculation about what causes this plateau in internal temperature, Dr. Greg Blonder, a physicist, recently discovered that it is actually caused by evaporation.

When large pieces of meat are cooked at a low temperature, water is released, evaporates, and cools on the surface of the meat, creating a stall in the internal temperature. The meat is, in effect, sweating the same way humans do.

How do you beat it? You could just wait. The stall zone can last up to six hours, so mow the lawn, watch the game, and come back to the brisket or pork shoulder later. Once the evaporative effect stops, the temperature in the meat will steadily increase again.

Or you can increase the cooking temperature of your meat. By raising the temperature to 275°, the stall doesn't last nearly as long as it would at lower temperatures.

But there is a better way- competition cooks refer to it as the "Texas Crutch". When the meat hits 150°, wrap it in foil with a splash bit of liquid (apple juice or beer are favorites) to finish cooking. Not only does this ensure the bark is a deep mahogany without being tough, the internal temperature cruises right through the stall zone and finishes in less time.

Smoking In 3 Easy Steps

The entire barbecue process can be reduced to three basic steps.

1. **Prepare the meat**
   - Decide if you will use a brine, marinade, or rub to maximize the flavor of your meat.
   - Prepare the brine, marinade, or rub and apply it to your meat prior to cooking.

2. **Cook the meat**
   - Cook each meat according to its desired internal temperature, using its estimated smoke time as a guide.
   - Decide if you want to use the "Texas Crutch" to cook your large cuts of meat faster. This involves wrapping the meat in aluminum foil with a splash of liquid once it reaches an internal temperature of 150° and allowing it to finish cooking.
   - If you are planning to apply a mop or sauce, you will want to begin to do so approximately one hour before the meat is finished.
   - Once your meat has achieved the appropriate internal temperature, remove it from the smoker.

3. **Let the cooked meat sit at room temperature** for fifteen to twenty-five minutes immediately after removing it from the smoker to allow it to cool and be easier to handle. Serve with sauce. Or not.

Seems simple enough, right? If it was, there wouldn't be pitmasters all over the country honing their craft. There wouldn't be as many styles of barbecue as there are Supreme Court justices. Every brisket from every smoker would taste the same. But do not let the prospect of navigating the barbecuing possibilities paralyze you into packing away the smoker for good. Just start with the basics.

Preparing Meat For the Smoker

There are four basic methods of preparing meat for the smoker - brining, marinating, injecting, and rubbing. All have virtues, all have vices. The method you choose is a matter of what tastes good to you. Some will create elaborate rubs and marinades, some will brine, and still others will only apply salt and pepper to their meat. Whichever you choose, it should enhance the flavor of the meat, not mask it.

1. Brining

Meat loses a lot of moisture during the cooking process. In fact, most meats lose around 30 percent of their weight during the cooking process. This can leave lean cuts dry and flavorless. According to a University of Georgia study, brining meat can reduce this moisture loss to as little as 15 percent.

How? When salt meets water, it creates a positively charged sodium ion and a negatively charged chloride ion. As the salty liquid is absorbed into the meat, there is less water on the surface of the meat, meaning there is less evaporation during cooking and the meat stays moist and juicy.

There are two generally accepted brining methods - wet brining, which uses a salt water solution and dry brining, which uses the same ingredients, minus the water. Which is better? It's tough to say. Both yield a well-seasoned end product, but some chefs consider wet brining a waste of water.

Regardless of the method you choose, do not over brine your meat. A 15 lb turkey can be effectively brined overnight, but a 3 pound chicken only needs 2-3 hours. A dry brined steak will be ready to cook in 30 minutes but a 6 lb dry brined pork butt can sit overnight in the fridge. A good rule of thumb is to let your meat brine no more than one hour per pound.

Remember: A wet brine is a delicate concoction of salt and water. Adding too much or too little of either ingredient can result in an imbalanced brine. Be sure to consider how much meat you need to brine -- generally, ½ cup of kosher salt to ½ gallon of water

Making a Wet Brine

No Heat Technique

This brining method is the simplest version to make.

1. Fill a container large enough to store the meat being used for the brine (a large pitcher, for example) with ½ gallon of water.
2. Stir in ½ cup of kosher salt until it completely dissolves into the water.
3. Add spices or aromatics to enhance your saltwater solution. Quartered onion, whole cloves of garlic, whole peppercorns, bay leaves, halved lemons or oranges, whole fennel bulbs or seeds all make great additions to a brine.

Over Heat Technique

1. Heat a gallon of water in a large pot over medium-high heat.
2. Stir in 1 cup of kosher salt until it dissolves completely.
3. Add other ingredients (crushed red pepper, garlic cloves, brown sugar, pepper, etc.) and let the solution come to a slow boil.
4. Reduce the heat to a simmer for about 15 minutes.
5. Turn off the heat and let the brine cool before setting it in the fridge.

DO

- Cool your brine between 33-39°F before submerging the meat. This ensures your meat stays out of the "danger zone" where bacteria growth accelerates.
- Use food-grade plastic or glass containers to brine your meat.
- Make enough brine solution so that the meat is completely submerged.
- Experiment with brine solutions and aromatics. You can even substitute part of the water with other liquids, such as beer, fruit juice, soda, etc.

DON'T

- Add too much salt. If the salt you added isn't dissolving completely, more water must be added to change the salt concentration.
- Let any part of the meat stick out of the brine.
- Reuse any brine solution. Discard any water after use and thoroughly clean the storage container.
- Brine your meat too long. Remember, no more than one hour per pound.

Dry Brining

A dry brine is made of the same ingredients as a wet brine, without the water. The question then becomes, how much of each ingredient do you use? A good rule of thumb is to use ½ teaspoon (tsp) salt per pound of meat. The rest becomes an issue of proportion. If you are dry brining an 8 pound pork butt, you would use 4 tsp of salt, then half as much of everything else - 2 tsp of pepper, 2 tsp of fresh thyme, 2 tsp of crushed red pepper flake, etc. The same rule applies for dry brining as wet - do not over brine your meat. One hour per pound is sufficient.

2. Marinades

A liquid mixture of oil, spices, and acid (usually vinegar or citrus) is considered a marinade. Meat is added to a marinade for 12 to 24 hours right before smoking to both flavor and tenderize it. Marinades are also often used as a "mop" to keep the surface of the meat moist and glazed and as an injection to flavor the meat beyond the surface. For marinade ideas, check out the recipe section.

3. Injecting

Injecting delicious flavor directly into the meat has become quite the rage among barbecue enthusiasts. Many barbecue competition champions have boasted that the secret to their success was injecting their meat with a suspension of spices, oil, and vinegar. Coating the outside of a thick piece of meat with a dry rub simply isn't going to get the thick inner parts to absorb that delicious flavor.

So let the barbecue "purists" complain about authenticity. Many of our favorite recipes today were made by breaking some rules, so don't feel bad about using modern tools to cook damn good meat!

What can you inject?

The wonderful answer to this question is that just about anything can be injected into meat. Fatty substances like butter or olive oil can deliver phenomenal flavor into the center of the meat, while full-fledged marinades take the whole process to a new level. The resulting experience from injecting is nothing short of tantalizing! You will need a "meat injector" (see our Tools of the Trade guide for more info).

1. Press down the plunger and fully submerge the needle into the marinade or liquid.
2. Pull the plunger back to fill the tube with the marinade or liquid.
3. Pierce the needle deep into the piece of meat and press the plunger down again slowly to release the liquid.
4. Remove the needle from the meat when all the liquid has been dispensed.

4. Rubbing

A mixture of spices and dried seasonings that is applied to the surface of meat is called a dry rub. It can be massaged into meat either the night before or right before firing up the meat in the smoker. Some folks claim that applying the rub several hours before cooking gets best results, but this might just be one of those old wives' tales.

Rubs can be applied directly to the outside of the meat. If cooking meats with the skin on, try seasoning the meat under the skin without tearing it off. Using a sticky substance like yellow mustard makes applying the rub a lot easier, and it is also a quintessential Southern barbecue custom. Cooking the mustard in high heat will destroy its tanginess, but it does help create a tasty outer crust. Consider using fats like butter or olive oil as an alternative to yellow mustard if you don't want to alter the flavor of your seasoning too much.

For more rub ideas, check out the "Awesome Rubs" section.

Cooking Techniques

While it is certainly possible to cook a piece of meat from start to finish on the smoker, it is by no means the only way. But first, it is important to understand some terms.

- **Indirect Grilling** - Large cuts of meat are big and tough, so they need to be cooked much longer. Indirect grilling is the perfect way to cook these types of meat without burning the outside before the insides are completely done. Also known as the "low and slow" cooking method, the fire burns on one or both sides of the meat rather than directly underneath it. The heat inside the grill or smoker circulates around the food, cooking it nice and evenly. The final result is juicy, tender barbecue.
- **Direct Grilling** - Hot and fast grilling is when food is cooked directly over the heat source. This method is best for smaller and thinner cuts of meat that tend to be tender. Searing is a type of direct grilling that locks in moisture by browning the outside of the meat; this is what causes grill marks. Opening and closing the air vent allows the chef to decrease or increase heat in the apparatus, respectively.
- **Dual Zone Grilling** - Setting up the grill to have both indirect and direct heat. This allows the cook to control how quickly their food cooks. Since different reactions happen at different times, having a hot, direct zone and a cooler, indirect zone on a grill gives you the chance to brown your food quickly then finish it at a lower temperature.
- **Searing or Browning** - Placing the meat in a hot, flat skillet to create the "Maillard Reaction". This happens when proteins and sugars in the meat meet high heat, creating golden, brown, and delicious food.

When using a smoker, it is possible to use a combination of methods to achieve the best possible flavor and texture in your big hunk of meat or poultry. Consider these possibilities:

- **Smo-fried Turkey** - After rubbing your turkey between the skin and meat with your favorite rub, smoke the bird at 250°F for 2 hours. Remove the turkey from the smoker and finish cooking in a 325°F peanut oil bath until the internal temperature of the thigh reaches 165°F. Not only with the skin be crispy and delicious, but the smoky flavor will have penetrated the meat without drying it out.
- **Smo-seared Ribeyes** - Rub your ribeye steaks with your favorite rub at least 30 minutes prior to cooking. Smoke until the steaks reach 120°F then place in a hot cast iron skillet with one tablespoon (Tbsp) of olive oil, over high heat, for 1-2 minutes on each side. Not only will the steaks have a luscious hint of smokiness, they will also have a delicious golden brown exterior.

Aluminum Foil Method (a.k.a. the "Texas Crutch" or "3-2-1 Method")

In order to combat "the stall" that large pieces of meat go through during the smoking process, and keep the meat succulent, the "Texas Crutch" or "3-2-1 method" of cooking should be used. During this process, the meat is smoked uncovered for three hours, or until the internal temperature reaches 150°F. It is then covered with aluminum foil and a splash of liquid (apple juice or beer are popular choices) for two hours. Finally, the remaining hour is spent uncovered at a higher temperature, being bathed in a mop sauce or barbecue sauce.

Contrary to popular belief, wrapping the meat in foil doesn't actually steam the meat. Instead, the meat is really being braised. Braising is a wet cooking method that starts with a high temperature to sear the food, then is finished in a covered pot with a small amount of liquid, at a low temperature. This technique actually cooks the meat faster and leaves it tender, juicy, and flavorful.

Mops & Sauces

Mops

A liquid that is brushed or sprayed onto the surface of meat is called a mop. Some folks say that it adds an extra layer of flavor while others say it can make the outside of the meat too soft. One problem with a mop that you must always remember is that the use of a mop requires the opening and closing of the smoker every hour, which results in an immediate drop in the internal temperature of the smoker.

How do you know when to use a mop?

There are certain instances when a mop will make a difference and ones where it will not really add anything to the recipe. For example, many people despise meat that is dried out from overcooking, so using a mop a few times while smoking can keep the outer part of the meat moist. Meats that have plenty of fat on the surface don't usually require a mop because the heat bastes this fat and causes it to pool into pockets of delicious flavor.

Sauces

There are four main types of barbecue sauces recognized in the world of amazing barbecued meat, and each one represents a major barbecue haven in the United States.

A barbecue sauce is generally considered a finishing sauce, so it is applied at the end of the smoking process. It is recommended that sauce be applied thirty to sixty minutes before the meat is done cooking.

Red Tomato Sauce: This ketchup-based sauce is found almost everywhere, but each region has its own exciting twist. Texans enjoy a Mexican-influenced spicy pepper version, while people from Tennessee make a sweet and sticky version made from either brown sugar or molasses

Yellow Mustard Sauce: This mustard-based sauce hails from South Carolina. The common yellow sauce is tangy and slightly sweetened from honey or brown sugar, but there are some spicy local versions floating around as well.

Clear Vinegar Sauce: This vinegar-based sauce is one of the oldest known sauces used to cook barbecue. It's a regional favorite in Virginia and North Carolina, and tends to contain hot peppers for a strong spicy and sour flavor.

White Mayonnaise Sauce: This mayonnaise-based sauce is so famous in Alabama that it is used in everything from dips and marinades. It's a well-balanced tangy sauce that comes in either a creamy or milky consistency, and typically only has four ingredients -- mayonnaise, vinegar, black pepper, and salt.

Black Worcestershire Sauce: This Worcestershire-based sauce is less commonly found compared to the other sauces. It's flavor draws from the salty and umami flavor of Worcestershire sauce, and it goes great with meats like lamb or mutton.

A Few Final Words on Barbecuing

1. This cannot be emphasized enough. Cook to temperature, not time. The recipes you will read in this book have smoking times. They are almost always given in ranges (i.e. 2-2.5 hours). Use your meat thermometer as your guide.

2. Do not leave your meat out at room temperature for longer than 1 hour. You are asking for bacteria trouble. Bringing your meat to room temperature will help it cook more evenly, but shoot for 30 minutes. That way if your team is on a hot streak when 30 minutes are up, you have a little leeway.

3. Wash everything that has touched raw meat as soon as the meat is in the smoker. The last thing you want is for the bacteria from the raw chicken you just put in the smoker to end up in someone's mouth. Wash your hands, the plate, the tongs, everything.

4. Minimize the number of times you open your smoker. There's a saying among pitmasters, "If you're lookin', it ain't cookin'." Every time you open the door of your smoker, you are adding cooking time.

5. If you are cooking chicken and intend to eat the skin, (a.k.a. chicken bacon) season it with the same rub you are using under the skin. You can thank me later.

6. Never, ever EVER cut into a piece of meat to see if it's done. If there is a knife by your smoker or grill, put it away. Use your thermometer.

7. The blackish stuff on the outside of your pork butt isn't burned. It's called bark. And it's delicious.

8. Don't throw away the chewy ends of the brisket. They're called "burnt ends" and they are spectacular in baked beans (see the recipe for "Burnt End Baked Beans").

9. Cheaper cuts of meat are ideal for the smoking beginner. They're foolproof ways to dip your toes into the world of barbecue. Even if you overcook them a little, they will still be delicious. But you won't. Because you read this book cover-to-cover. Right?

10. It's time to get over eating your steaks anywhere past medium doneness. Every time you tell a waitress "well done" a fairy dies. Maybe not, but you are sacrificing flavor and texture every time. Stop it. Save the fairies.

11. The pink juice coming out of your steak is not blood. It's water and myoglobin.

12. If your meat is finished before you are ready to eat, don't fear. Fill a small cooler ¼ of the way full with very hot tap water for 10 minutes then pour it out. (Please use it for another purpose rather than just dumping it down the drain.) Wrap the meat tightly in aluminum foil and place it in the empty cooler. Keep the lid shut and it will stay warm until you are ready to eat.

13. Don't rely solely on sauce to season your meat. Even if you have an award winning barbecue sauce, don't skip the chance to add flavor prior to cooking. A little salt and pepper can go a long way to enhancing your finished product.

14. Remember, barbecuing is not meant to be a stressful experience. Relax. Have a tasty beverage. Take a nap in the hammock. It will all be okay.

RECIPES

Now that you are an expert on the Masterbuilt® smoker and now that you are on your way to a degree in food science, it is time to get down to the nitty gritty, the reason you bought this book. Recipes.

That word sounds so benign, when in reality you hold in your hand the holy grail of barbecue cookery. .

First we'll talk preparation. You will find a variety of tantalizing rubs, and sauces, many of which can be used as marinades, to go with every dish imaginable. From Korean influenced sauces to traditional rubs, there is something for everyone in these pages.

All of the rubs can be made ahead of time unless otherwise noted. When you are ready to smoke your meat, simply sprinkle the rub onto the meat and rub (hence the name) it into the flesh and skin. This can be done 30 minutes in advance or a day in advance. The longer it sits, the more flavorful the finished product. But don't let a late start make you skip this step. 30 minutes will still have an effect on the flavor.

Sauces are meant to be applied 30-60 minutes before the meat is finished cooking, unless otherwise noted. Sauces tend to have a high sugar content and are likely to burn if applied too soon. There is nothing worse than spending hours on a slab of ribs only to ruin them by slathering on the sauce too soon. Who are we kidding? We'll still eat them.

Next we'll put it all together. We figured it would be easier to not only organize the book into beef, pork, etc., but also to include a "core recipe" then the variations on that theme. Once you can smoke a brisket, making pastrami is a breeze. After you have eaten your fill of that brisket, we'll show you how to turn it into delicious breakfast fajitas for a second meal that will knock your socks off.

Most importantly, understand that these recipes are merely a jumping off point. Try them out the way they are written the first time. Then the next time, add a little more of this or a little less of that to your taste. You may be surprised to discover that your long-standing feud with Chinese five spice powder was cured by our Asian Rub liberally applied to St. Louis style ribs slathered with our Chinese Barbecue Sauce.

Beef

PERFECTLY SMOKED BRISKET

Pastrami
Hot N' Smoky Breakfast Fajitas
Southwestern Smoked Chili
Rowdy Cowboy Sandwich

THE ULTIMATE BARBECUE MEATLOAF

Red Scorpion Sting Meatloaf
French Kiss Meatloaf

BIG & BOLD SMOKED BURGERS

Smoked Cheesy Burgers
Smoked Pastrami Burgers
Smoked Burgers with Seared Avocado

3-INGREDIENT SMOKED CHUCK ROAST

Pulled Beef Sandwich
Shredded Beef Enchiladas

MIGHTY MEATY BEEF TENDERLOIN

Tenderloin Kebabs
Perfectly Smoked Filet Mignon
Garlic & Onion Tenderloin

PERFECTLY SMOKED PRIME RIB

Prime Rib Flatbreads
Prime Rib Pizza

PERFECTLY SMOKED BEEF RIBS

LIP-SMACKIN' SHORT RIBS

"Quick" Short Rib Osso Bucco

PERFECTLY SMOKED BRISKET

Serves: 8-10 | **Preparation Time:** 25 min

Brisket is a versatile slab of beef, perfect for beginner smokers. Be sure to purchase a brisket with a layer of fat and smoke it fat-side up.

Estimated Smoke Time: 8-10 Hours (1 hour per lb.)
Smoke Temp: 250°F
Try these wood chips: Cherry, hickory or mesquite

Ingredients:

Meat	Spices	Sauces
❏ 8-10 lb. whole brisket, trimmed	❏ Basic beef rub	❏ Jeff's Mop Sauce

Preparation:

Meat
1. Set the brisket in an aluminum pan, fat side-up.
2. Inject the mop sauce into the meat in one inch increments.
3. Cover the aluminum pan and refrigerate for at least 6 hours or overnight.
4. Move the brisket to a clean aluminum pan and liberally apply the basic beef rub to the meat.
5. Let the brisket come to room temperature in the aluminum pan for 30 minutes as the smoker preheats to 250°F.

Smoking:
1. Set the brisket directly on the smoker grate with the aluminum pan on the rack beneath it.
2. Begin checking the internal temperature of the brisket after 8 hours. Remove the brisket from the smoker when the internal temperature reaches 190°F.
3. Let the meat rest for 15-20 minutes before carving.

PASTRAMI

Serves: 6 | **Preparation Time:** Active, 10 min. Passive, 4 days plus smoke time.
Estimated Cook Time: 10-12 hours

A pastrami sandwich on rye at Katz's Deli is a quintessential New York experience. Rooted in Jewish tradition, pastrami is cured, rubbed, smoked, then steamed. While it may seem like a lot of work for a measly sandwich, once you master pastrami, you can bring New York to you anytime.

Estimated Smoke Time: 8-10 hours
Smoke Temp: 250°F
Try these wood chips: Cherry, pecan, oak, or apple

Ingredients:

Meat	Cure	Spices/Rub
❑ 1 (12-lb.) whole beef brisket	❑ 3 Tbsp garlic, granulated ❑ 2 Tbsp pickling spice ❑ 2 Tbsp ground coriander ❑ ¼ cup curing salt	❑ 3 Tbsp black pepper, coarsely ground ❑ 1 Tbsp coriander seeds, toasted and ground ❑ 1 tsp garlic, granulated ❑ 1 cup water

Preparation:
1. Wash the brisket and pat-dry.
2. Trim the fat evenly across the surface of the brisket, leaving ½ inch of fat on the meat.
3. In a bowl, combine all cure ingredients. Coat the brisket entirely with the cure.
4. Place the cured brisket in a 2-gallon resealable bag. Refrigerate it for 4 days, turning the brisket 1-2 times per day.
5. After 4 days, remove the brisket from the bag. Wash it well and pat-dry.
6. In a mixing bowl, mix together all of the rub ingredients.
7. Coat the brisket evenly with the rub.
8. Let it sit for at room temperature for 30 minutes while the smoker comes to temperature (250°F).

Smoking:
1. Set the brisket directly on the smoker grate, fat side up.
2. Smoke the meat for 4-5 hours, or until the internal temperature registers 165°F.
3. Remove the brisket from the smoker.
4. Wrap the brisket tightly in aluminum foil, adding 1 cup of water before sealing the foil.
5. Place the pastrami back to the smoker and cook until the internal temperature registers 190°F.
6. For best results, let the pastrami rest for 20-30 minutes before slicing.

HOT N' SMOKY BREAKFAST FAJITAS

Serves: 5 | **Preparation Time:** 20 min

If you have a lot of leftover smoked brisket from yesterday's barbecue, then this recipe is a good way to use it up. Chop up the leftover brisket meat, add a few ingredients, and prepare to be amazed at this take on breakfast fajitas.

Ingredients:

Fajitas	Other
❑ 1 Tbsp extra-virgin olive oil	❑ 10 (8-inch) flour tortillas
❑ 4 cups perfectly smoked brisket, chopped	*Garnishes*
❑ 2 red bell peppers, julienned	❑ Pico de gallo
❑ 1 small red onion, julienned	❑ Shredded Cheese
❑ 1 large jalapeno pepper, seeded and julienned	❑ Sour Cream
❑ 2 Tbsp butter	❑ Guacamole
❑ 10 eggs, scrambled	

Preparation:

Tortillas

1. In a frying pan over low heat warm the tortillas one at a time, approximately 15 seconds per side.
2. Set aside, covered with a warm towel.

Fajitas

1. In a separate pan over medium-high heat, add oil, onion, bell pepper, and jalapeno.
2. Saute the vegetables until they are soft and the onions begin to brown, about 10 minutes.
3. Add in the chopped smoked brisket and saute for another 2 minutes.
4. Transfer the vegetable and meat mixture into a bowl and set aside.
5. In the same pan, add the butter and allow it to melt and become foamy.
6. Add the eggs and reduce the heat to medium low.
7. Stir the eggs as they set, allowing them to cook to a firm, creamy consistency.
8. Just before they are finished, add the meat and vegetable mixture and allow it to warm through.

To assemble: Top a warm tortilla with the egg and brisket mixture. Garnish with cheese, pico de gallo, sour cream or guacamole.

SOUTHWESTERN SMOKED CHILI

Serves: 6 | **Preparation Time:** 10 min.
Estimated Cook Time: 45 minutes

Braving the cold will be much more delightful with a hot bowl of beef chili from leftover smoked brisket. This recipe comes together quickly with a few items in your fridge and pantry, making it ideal for busy days.

Perfectly Smoked Brisket Recipes

Ingredients:

Chili	Spices
❑ 1 Tbsp extra-virgin olive oil	❑ 1 Tbsp Chili Rub
❑ 1 ½ cups onion, diced	
❑ 1 ½ cups green pepper, diced	
❑ 1 tbs. minced garlic	
❑ 3 cups water	
❑ 2 Tbsp tomato paste	
❑ 1 14.5-ounce can tomato sauce	
❑ 2 lbs. perfectly smoked brisket, chopped	
❑ 3 cans beans, any variety, rinsed and drained	

Preparation:

1. In a large pot, heat oil over medium heat.
2. Add onion and green pepper and cook until soft.
3. Add minced garlic and tomato paste and cook until tomato paste turns brick red. Add water and stir.
4. Add chili rub, tomato sauce, brisket and beans.
5. Simmer uncovered for 30 minutes or until the chili begins to thicken.

ROWDY COWBOY SANDWICH

Serves: 4 | **Preparation Time:** 10 min

This rowdy cowboy sandwich is the perfect sandwich for surely a must-try. With just four ingredients, it makes the perfect dinner-on-the-go.

Ingredients:

Meat	Other
❏ Perfectly smoked brisket, chopped	❏ 8 thick bread slices ❏ 4 pepper jack cheese slices ❏ pickled onions ❏ pickled jalapeño slices ❏ Classic Texas Barbecue Sauce

Preparation:
1. Preheat the broiler in your oven.
2. On a cookie sheet, lay out bread slices, topping half with the cheese.
3. Toast bread slices for 1-2 min under the broiler, or until cheese melts.
4. Add a layer of warm chopped brisket to half of the slices.
5. Squeeze a drizzle of Classic Texas Barbecue Sauce over the meat.
6. Top with pickled onions and jalapeño slices.
7. Top with the remaining toasted bread.

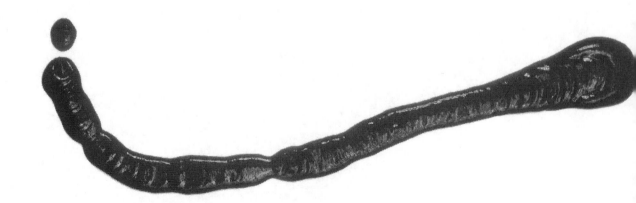

THE ULTIMATE
BARBECUE MEATLOAF

Serves: 4 | **Preparation Time:** 10-15 min

Meat loaf is the one dish that everyone has a recipe for, and no one has put in the smoker. Smoked meatloaf is meaty and savory, while the smoke adds a twist to this comfort classic. This particular recipe is also made more flavorful with the sweet and smoky barbecue sauce added at the end.

Estimated Smoke Time: 1 ½ - 2 hours
Smoke Temp: 275°F
Try these wood chips: Cherry, hickory or mesquite

Ingredients:

Meat	Other Ingredients	Sauce
❑ 2 lbs. ground chuck	❑ 2 Tbsp Worcestershire sauce ❑ 1 small yellow onion, grated ❑ 1 clove garlic, finely minced ❑ 1 small bell pepper, finely diced ❑ 1 cup bread crumbs ❑ ½ cup milk ❑ 1 egg, lightly beaten ❑ 1 Tbsp Basic Barbecue Rub	❑ 1 cup Honey Chipotle Bold Barbecue Sauce

Preparation:
1. In a bowl, combine bread crumbs and milk and allow the bread to become soggy.
2. Drain the bread and mix with the remaining ingredients and ½ cup of the barbecue sauce, reserving the rest for the top. Do not overwork the meat. No one likes a tough meatloaf.
3. Form the mixture into a 5"x9" rectangular log in the middle of a 9"x13" aluminum foil pan.

Smoking:
1. Set the pan with the meatloaf on the smoker grate.
2. Smoke the meatloaf until it reaches an internal temperature of 155°F.
3. Remove the meatloaf from the smoker and brush it with the remaining barbecue sauce.
4. Return the meatloaf to the smoker for another 20-30 minutes or until the internal temperature reaches 160°F.
5. Let it rest for a 5-10 minutes before slicing them. Serve.

RED SCORPION STING MEATLOAF

Serves: 6 | **Preparation Time:** 10-15 min

This meatloaf variation will give your tongue a good beating. But oh, it hurts so good.

Estimated Smoke Time: 2 - 2 ½ hours
Smoke Temp: 275°F
Try these wood chips: Cherry, hickory or apple

Ingredients:

Meat	Rub	Other
❑ 2 lbs ground chuck	❑ 1-3 Tbsp Habanero rub	❑ 6-7 medium mushrooms, finely chopped ❑ 3 eggs ❑ 1 ½ cups fresh white breadcrumbs ❑ 1 jalapeno, finely chopped ❑ 1 medium onion, minced ❑ ½ cup Frank's Buffalo Sauce

Preparation:
1. In a large bowl, mix together the ground chuck, onion, jalapeno, mushrooms, eggs, ¼ cup of the Frank's Buffalo Sauce, and the bread crumbs.
2. After mixing, shape the meatloaf into a 5" x 9" rectangle.
3. Using a knife or any sharp object, make holes at the bottom of a 9"x 13" disposable aluminum pan, approximately 1 hole per square inch so the grease and juices will easily drain from the pan as the meatloaf is smoked.
4. Set the loaf in the prepared aluminum pan and sprinkle with as much rub as you dare.

Smoking:
1. Set the aluminum pan with the meatloaf on the smoker grate.
2. Use a drip pan to catch the grease and juices as the meatloaf is smoked.
3. Smoke the meatloaf for 1 ½ - 2 hours or until it reaches an internal temperature of 155°F
4. Remove the meatloaf from the smoker and brush with the remaining hot sauce.
5. Return the meatloaf to the smoker an additional 20-30 minutes or until it reaches an internal temperature of 160°F.
6. Allow the meatloaf to rest for 15 minutes before slicing.

FRENCH KISS MEATLOAF

Serves: 6 | **Preparation Time:** 10-15 min

If French onion soup and meatloaf had a baby, this is what it would look like. Stuffed with caramelized onions, this meatloaf is sure to please the most discerning palates.

Estimated Smoke Time: 2-2 ½ hours
Smoke Temp: 275°F
Try these wood chips: Oak, pecan, or mesquite

Ingredients:

Meat	Other	Sauce
❑ 2 lbs. ground beef	❑ 2 Tbsp extra-virgin olive oil ❑ 2 large onions, thinly sliced ❑ 2 eggs, lightly beaten ❑ 2 garlic cloves, minced ❑ 1 cup fresh white breadcrumbs ❑ ¼ cup whole milk ❑ dash of tabasco sauce ❑ 1 Tbsp English Pub Rub	❑ ½ cup Balsamic Barbecue Sauce

Preparation:
1. In a large bowl, mix together breadcrumbs and milk, set aside.
2. In a large skillet, heat the olive oil over medium heat.
3. Add the onions and reduce heat to medium low. Allow the onions to cook slowly, first becoming translucent, then caramelizing. Once the onions are caramelized, set aside to cool.
4. To the breadcrumb mixture, add the ground beef, garlic, eggs, tabasco sauce, and English Pub Rub. Use your hands to thoroughly combine.
5. Divide the mixture in half, forming two 5"x9" loaves.
6. Transfer one loaf to a disposable aluminum pan.
7. Spread the caramelized onions down the center of the meatloaf, leaving a half-inch rim around the edge of the loaf.
8. Lay the remaining loaf on top, lightly pressing the edges to seal the onions inside.

Smoking:
1. Set the pan with the meatloaf on the smoker grate.
2. Smoke the meatloaf for 1 ½ - 2 hours or until the internal temperature reaches 155°F.
3. Brush the meatloaf with the Balsamic Barbecue sauce and return it to the smoker for 20-30 minutes or until the meatloaf reaches 160°F.
4. Remove the meatloaf from the smoker and let it sit for 5-10 minutes before slicing.

BIG & BOLD SMOKED BURGERS

Serves: 2 | **Preparation Time:** 25 min

The secret to big and bold smoked burgers is smoking the burgers first, and then searing them for a few minutes in a cast iron pan in butter. This creates a nice crust and a very rich flavor. Add bacon, sharp cheddar cheese, and a few veggies and you have taken a classic burger to the next level.

Estimated Smoke Time: 15-30 minutes
Smoke Temp: 275°F
Try these wood chips: Cherry, hickory or mesquite

Ingredients:

Meat	Spices	Other	Garnish
❏ 1 lb. ground chuck or equivalent 80/20 ground beef	❏ 1 (1-oz.) packet dry ranch dressing mix ❏ 1 tsp Basic Beef Rub	❏ 2 Tbsp butter, unsalted ❏ 2 slices sharp cheddar cheese ❏ 2 slices cooked bacon ❏ 2 white hamburger buns, toasted	❏ mayonnaise ❏ lettuce ❏ ripe tomato, sliced

Preparation:
1. Preheat the smoker to 275°F.
2. Using a medium-sized non-reactive bowl, mix together the ground beef, dry ranch dressing mix, and beef rub and form into two patties.

Smoking:
1. Put the patties in a shallow aluminum pan and place the pan on the preheated smoker.
2. Smoke the patties until they reach an internal temperature of 130°F.
3. Remove the burgers from the smoker.

Finishing:
1. Heat a cast iron skillet over medium high heat for 5-7 minutes.
2. Remove the pan from the heat and add butter, swirling the pan to make sure the butter does not burn.
3. Return the pan to the heat and add the hamburgers to the pan.
4. Spoon the melted butter over the hamburgers for 2 minutes.
5. Flip the hamburgers and immediately top with the cheese.
6. Turn off the heat and lightly cover the hamburgers with aluminum foil, allowing the residual heat to melt the cheese and finish caramelizing the hamburger.
7. Dress the toasted buns with the condiments of your choice and top with the luscious smo-fried hamburger.

SMOKED CHEESY BURGERS

Serves: 2 | Preparation Time: 25 mins

Think of this like an inside out cheeseburger with extra cheesy goodness. The combination of cream cheese, American cheese, and blue cheese makes these burgers extra gooey..

Estimated Smoke Time: 20-30 minutes
Smoke Temp: 250°F
Try these wood chips: Cherry or apple

Ingredients:

Meat	Cheese Filling	Other
❑ 1 lb ground chuck or other 80/20 ground beef ❑ 2 tsp Basic Beef Rub	❑ 1 onion, thinly sliced ❑ 1 Tbsp extra-virgin olive oil ❑ 2 oz. cream cheese, softened ❑ 2 oz shredded sharp cheddar cheese ❑ 1 Tbsp blue cheese, crumbled	❑ 2 hamburger buns, toasted ❑ 2 slices bacon, cooked ❑ 2 Tbsp choice of barbecue sauce

Preparation:

Meat
1. Preheat the smoker to 250°F.
2. In a medium skillet, heat olive oil over medium heat. Add onions and cook slowly until onions turn translucent then caramelize, around 20 minutes.
3. In a bowl, combine cream cheese, sharp cheddar cheese, and blue cheese.
4. Form hamburger into four patties of equal size.
5. Place half of the cheese mixture the center of one patty. Top with an additional patty and seal around the edges. Repeat for the other hamburger.
6. Season both hamburgers with the basic beef rub and place in a shallow aluminum foil pan.

Smoking:
1. Place the pan on the preheated smoker.
2. Smoke the burgers until they reach an internal temperature of 155°F.
3. Remove the burgers from the smoker and allow to rest for 5 minutes. The internal temperature will continue to increase to 160°F.

Assembly:
1. Spread barbecue sauce over the top of each hamburger bun.
2. Place hamburgers on the toasted bottom bun. Top with bacon and the other bun.
3. Devour next to a pile of napkins.

SMOKED PASTRAMI BURGERS

Serves: 2 | **Preparation Time:** 10 min

Remember the pastrami from the brisket section? This would be a great way to use it. But don't let a lack of homemade pastrami deter you from making this burger. Deli pastrami from your local grocery store will be just as delicious.

Estimated Smoke Time: 20-30 minutes
Smoke Temp: 250°F
Try these wood chips: Cherry or apple

Ingredients:

Meat	Other
❏ 1 lb ground chuck or other 80/20 ground beef	❏ 2 hamburger buns
❏ 2 tsp Basic Beef Rub	❏ 4 Tbsp mayonnaise
❏ 4 oz thinly sliced pastrami	❏ 2 Tbsp ketchup
	❏ 1 tsp pickle relish
	❏ 2 slices Swiss cheese
	❏ 1-2 leaves of lettuce
	❏ 2 slices tomato

Preparation:
1. Preheat the smoker to 250°F.
2. Form hamburger into two patties and place in a shallow aluminum pan and season both sides with Basic Beef Rub.

Smoking:
1. Place the pan in the smoker and cook 15-20 minutes or until the internal temperature reaches 150°F.
2. Remove the burgers from the smoker and top with pastrami.
3. Return to the smoker until the internal temperature of the hamburgers reaches 160°F.
4. Remove from smoker and top with cheese. Cover lightly with aluminum foil and allow the burgers to rest for 5 minutes.

Assembly:
1. In a small bowl, combine mayonnaise, ketchup and relish.
2. Spread the mayonnaise mixture on all of the toasted buns.

Top bottom bun with burger, garnishes of your choice, and the remaining bun.

SMOKED BURGERS WITH SEARED AVOCADO

Serves: 2 | **Preparation Time:** 25 min

There can be a lot of variations when it comes to smoked burgers, but this recipe is a sure stand-out. Who would have thought to sear avocado slices? The trick is to use a small skillet and a very firm avocado. This makes this recipe ideal for those unripe avocados you had to buy at the last minute. (Not that we've ever done that.)

Estimated Smoke Time: 20-30 minutes

Smoke Temp: 250°F

Try these wood chips: Cherry or apple

Ingredients:

Meat	Other
❏ 1 lb ground chuck or other 80/20 ground beef ❏ 2 tsp Basic Beef Rub	❏ 1 Tbsp olive oil, for brushing on avocado ❏ ½ of a firm-ripe avocado, pitted, peeled, and cut lengthwise into 4 (1/3 inch thick) slices ❏ 2 hamburger buns ❏ 2 Tbsp mayonnaise ❏ 1 tsp Sriracha ❏ 2 slices bacon, cooked ❏ 1-2 leaves of lettuce ❏ 2 slices tomato

Preparation:
1. Preheat the smoker to 250°F.
2. Form hamburger into two patties and place in a shallow aluminum pan and season both sides with Basic Beef Rub.

Smoking:
1. Place the pan in the smoker and cook 20-30 minutes or until the internal temperature reaches 160°F.
2. Remove the burgers from the smoker and allow to rest for 5 minutes.

Assembly:
1. Heat a small skillet over medium-high heat.
2. Brush both sides of the avocado slices with olive oil. Season with salt and pepper.
3. Place avocado in the skillet and sear for 1-2 minutes on each side.
4. In a small bowl combine mayonnaise and sriracha.
5. Spread one bun with sriracha mayonnaise mixture. Top with a hamburger, desired garnishes, and the remaining bun.

3-INGREDIENT SMOKED CHUCK ROAST

Serves: 6-8 | **Preparation Time:** 10 min

Brisket is a versatile slab of beef, perfect for beginner smokers. Be sure to purchase a brisket with a layer of fat and smoke it fat-side up.

Estimated Smoke Time: 6-8 hours
Smoke Temp: 225°F
Try these wood chips: Cherry, hickory or mesquite

Ingredients:

Meat	Other
❑ 4-6 lb. chuck roast	❑ 1 Tbsp kosher salt
	❑ 1 Tbsp black pepper, coarsely ground

Preparation:
1. Pat the roast dry with a paper towel.
2. Rub salt and pepper onto the entire roast.
3. Let it sit for 30-40 minutes at room temperature while preheating the smoker to 225°F.

Smoking:
1. Set the roast directly on the smoker grate.
2. Smoke until the internal temperature of the roast reaches 180°F.
3. Let it sit for a 5-10 minutes to cool before carving.

PULLED BEEF SANDWICH

Serves: 8-10 | **Preparation Time:** 30 min

Pulled beef sandwiches are the heart of true barbecue, and this one is made tastier by using deli rolls instead of bland ol' regular bread. Think of this sandwich like a beef dip rather than a barbecue sandwich, a perfect distraction from the ordinary.

Ingredients:

Meat	Sauce	Other
❑ 4-6 lb. Smoked Chuck Roast	❑ 2 cups beef broth ❑ 2 Tbsp fresh rosemary, minced ❑ 1 tsp black pepper, coarsely ground	❑ 3 Tbsp butter ❑ 2 yellow onions, sliced ❑ 10-12 deli rolls, buttered, toasted ❑ 1 (16-oz.) jar pepperoncini

Preparation:
1. Using 2 forks, shred the roast. Set aside.
2. In a medium saucepan, combine beef broth, rosemary, and pepper.
3. Bring the sauce to a simmer and add the smoked chuck roast to warm through.
4. Meanwhile, melt butter in a large skillet over medium heat. Add onions and saute until they become translucent, then caramelize, around 20 minutes.
5. Pull meat from the sauce and place on a toasted deli roll. Top with caramelized onions and sliced pepperoncini.
6. Serve sandwiches with small cups of the sauce for dipping.

SHREDDED BEEF ENCHILADAS

Serves: 4-6 | **Preparation Time:** 10 min

A good way to use up smoked chuck roast is to make it into beef enchiladas. The shredded roast meat blends nicely with the hot and spicy sauce. This one is super easy and will be a sure hit with your family and friends.

Estimated Smoke Time: 45-60 minutes
Smoke Temp: 275°F
Try these wood chips: Cherry, hickory or mesquite

Ingredients:

Meat	Sauce	Other
❏ 1 lb. Smoked Chuck Roast	❏ 4 dried pasilla chiles, stemmed and seeded ❏ 1-2 dried chipotle chiles, stemmed and seeded ❏ 2 Tbsp extra-virgin olive oil ❏ 1 small yellow onion, chopped ❏ 4 garlic cloves, chopped ❏ 1 tsp ground cumin ❏ ½ tsp oregano	❏ J12 corn tortillas ❏ 4 garlic cloves, minced ❏ 2 cups cheddar cheese, shredded ❏ 1 Tbsp vegetable oil ❏ 1 tsp ground cumin ❏ ½ medium yellow onion, diced ❏ 1 Tbsp salt and pepper, to taste

Preparation:

1. Using 2 forks, shred the chuck roast. Set aside.
2. In a large skillet, toast the chipotle and pasilla chiles on high heat, about 1 minute per side or until they start to become fragrant.
3. Add enough water to the pan until the chiles are just covered.
4. Allow the mixture to simmer for 10-15 minutes or until the chiles become soft.
5. Drain the chiles. reserving the water mixture.
6. In the same pan, add olive oil, onion, and garlic and allow the vegetables to become soft and translucent.
7. Combine the rehydrated chiles, the vegetable mixture, and enough of the reserved water in a blender to make a smooth sauce.
8. Season with cumin, oregano, and salt and pepper to taste.
9. Mix ¼ cup of the sauce with the meat.
10. In the same skillet over low heat, warm one tortilla until it is pliable.
11. Spoon 2 Tbsp of meat in the center of the tortilla and top with 1 Tbsp cheese.
12. Roll the tortilla around the mixture and place in a greased 9"x13" pan. Repeat with the remaining tortillas.
13. Pour sauce over the finished tortilla rolls and top with any remaining cheese.
14. Cover and place in the smoker 45-60 minutes or until the enchiladas are thoroughly warm. (This can also be done in a 350 degree oven for 30 minutes.)

MIGHTY MEATY BEEF TENDERLOIN

Serves: 12 | **Preparation Time:** overnight

Beef tenderloin is soft and buttery in texture but doesn't have a lot of beefy flavor. By smoking it to a medium rare, the natural beef flavors are amplified, making it a delicious choice for a special occasion.

Estimated Smoke Time: 4-6 hours
Smoke Temp: 275°F
Try these wood chips: Cherry, hickory or mesquite

Ingredients:

Meat	Marinade
❏ 4 lb. beef tenderloin roast	❏ Barbecue Beef Mop

Preparation:
1. Using a paper or kitchen towel, pat-dry the tenderloin roast.
2. Place the roast into 2 cups of Barbecue Beef Mop in a zip top bag. Refrigerate overnight.
3. The next day, remove the roast from the marinade and pat dry.
4. Let it sit at room temperature while preheating the smoker to 275°F.

Smoking:
1. Place the tenderloin directly on the smoker's grates.
2. Smoke to an internal temperature of 135°F for medium rare.
3. Allow the meat to rest for 20-30 minutes before carving. Slice the roast and serve.

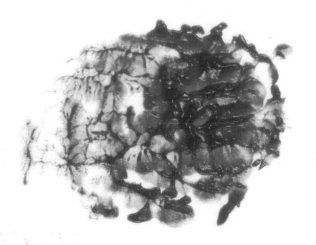

TENDERLOIN KEBABS

Serves: 4-6 | **Preparation Time:** 40 min

Kebabs are a great way to take advantage of the texture of the tenderloin while applying bold flavors. Serve these kebabs with naan for a delicious Middle-Eastern meal!

Estimated Smoke Time: 30-60 minutes
Smoke Temp: 275°F
Try these wood chips: Cherry, hickory or mesquite

Ingredients:

Meat	Marinade	Other
❏ 2 lbs beef tenderloin, trimmed and cubed into 2 inch cubes	❏ Double batch of North African Rub	❏ 2 Zucchini, cut into 1 inch rounds ❏ 1 lb button mushrooms ❏ 2 bell peppers, cut into 2 inch pieces ❏ 1 onion, cut into 2 inch pieces ❏ 8 oz cherry tomatoes ❏ Skewers, soaked in water

Preparation:
1. Place cold tenderloin chunks and half of the rub in a large zip top bag. Massage thoroughly and allow to sit for 30 minutes.
2. In a separate zip top bag, combine the remaining rub and vegetables and allow to sit for 30 minutes.
3. Preheat the smoker to 275°F.
4. Thread meat onto skewers, leaving a space between the chunks.
5. On separate skewers, thread alternating vegetables.

Smoking:
1. Place the skewers on the smoker grates and smoke until the meat registers 135°F.
2. Remove the skewers and serve immediately.

PERFECTLY SMOKED FILET MIGNON

Serves: 12 | Preparation Time: 15 min

When a beef tenderloin is cut into steaks, they are known as filet mignon. These prized cuts of meat are known for their texture, but our rub will make them known for their flavor as well.

Estimated Smoke Time: 2-3 Hours (30 min per lb.)
Smoke Temp: 275°F
Try these wood chips: Cherry, hickory or mesquite

Ingredients:

Meat	Spices	Sauces
❏ 4 lb beef tenderloin, trimmed	❏ 2-3 sprigs fresh thyme ❏ 2 shallots, peeled and chopped ❏ ½ cup chives, chopped	❏ ½ cup your favorite barbecue sauce - we like our Balsamic Barbecue Sauce for this ❏ 2 Tbsp butter ❏ 2 tsp Worcestershire sauce

Preparation:

Sauce
1. Heat the butter in a small pan over medium heat till it melts.
2. Toss in shallots and herbs into the warm butter.
3. Add the barbecue sauce and reduce heat to low.
4. Keep stirring the barbecue butter sauce to keep it from solidifying.

Meat
1. Cut ¾ of the way through the tenderloin to make steaks 1-2 inches thick.
2. Lay the partially sliced tenderloin across the bottom of an aluminum baking dish to let the strips open.
3. Gently pour the barbecue butter sauce into each flap to baste the tenderloin generously.
4. Let the basted tenderloin come to room temperature as the smoker preheats to 275°F.

Smoking:
1. Set the pan with the tenderloin directly on the smoker grate when the desired smoke temperature has been reached.
2. Smoke the meat until the internal temperature of the thickest steak comes to 135°F.
3. Let the meat rest for 5-10 minutes before carving.

GARLIC & ONION TENDERLOIN

Serves: 8-10 | **Preparation Time:** Active - 10 min; Passive - Overnight

The simplicity of the garlic and onion flavor in this smoked tenderloin recipe works perfectly as it complements the mild beefy flavor of the meat.

Estimated Smoke Time: 4-6 hours
Smoke Temp: 275°F
Try these wood chips: Mesquite

Ingredients:

Meat	Rub	Other
❑ 4 lbs. beef tenderloin	❑ 8 garlic cloves, chopped ❑ 1 large onion, roughly chopped ❑ ¼ cup black pepper, coarsely ground ❑ 2 Tbsp fresh lemon juice ❑ 1 tsp kosher salt ❑ ¼ tsp cayenne pepper	❑ 1 cup Jeff's Mop Water ❑ ¼ cup favorite barbecue sauce

Preparation:
1. In a food processor, pulse rub ingredients together until a paste forms.
2. Wash the tenderloin and pat dry.
3. Cover the meat with the rub, place in a zip top bag, and refrigerate overnight, for best results.
4. The next day, remove the meat from the fridge at least 30 minutes before smoking to allow the meat to come up to room temperature.
5. Preheat the smoker to 275°F.

Smoking:
1. Set the tenderloin directly on the smoker grate.
2. Smoke the meat until it reaches an internal temperature of 110°F.
3. Baste the meat on both sides with Jeff's Mop Water.
4. When the roast reaches 130°F, brush on your preferred barbecue sauce.
5. Return the roast to the smoker until it reaches 135°F for medium rare.
6. Remove from the smoker and let it sit for 15-20 minutes before carving. Serve.

PERFECTLY SMOKED PRIME RIB

Serves: 8-10 | **Preparation Time:** 6-7 hours

Smoked prime rib will have neighbors peeking over your backyard fence, wondering what the tantalizing aroma is. Put them out of their misery and invite them over. This recipe is very versatile. Substitute any of our amazing rubs and skip the marinade for a completely different, but equally delicious flavor.

Estimated Smoke Time: 5 hours

Smoke Temp: 230°F

Try these wood chips: Cherry, hickory or mesquite

Ingredients:

Meat	Rub	Marinade
❏ 5 lb. prime rib roast, well marbled	❏ 1 ½ Tbsp onion powder ❏ 1 ½ Tbsp garlic powder ❏ 1 Tbsp kosher salt ❏ 1 Tbsp black pepper, coarsely ground	❏ 1 recipe Everything Basting Sauce

Preparation:

1. Using a clean paper or kitchen towel, pat-dry the roast.
2. Place the roast in an aluminum pan and inject the Everything Basting Sauce into all surfaces of the roast.
3. Place the roast in the refrigerator for at least 6 hours. For best results, refrigerate it overnight.
4. Remove the roast from the fridge, and discard any remaining marinade from the pan.
5. In a separate bowl, mix together all rub ingredients.
6. Pour the rub onto the roast and use your hands to coat the meat evenly.
7. Let the roast sit at room temperature while preheating the smoker to 230°F.

Smoking:

1. Set the roasting pan on the smoker grate.
2. Smoke the roast until the internal temperature reaches 135°F for medium rare, 145 for medium.
3. Allow the roast to rest, covered for 30-45 minutes.
4. Carve the roast and serve with pan drippings poured over the meat.

PRIME RIB FLATBREAD

Serves: 4-6 | **Preparation Time:** 45 min

Use your smoker as an oven? Sure! Of course these flatbreads can be made on a traditional grill or in the oven, but why not infuse them with a little smoke? Use a light wood, like alder or fruit wood for a kiss of sweet smoke to this delicious appetizer

Estimated Smoke Time: 8-10 Hours (1 hour per lb.)
Smoke Temp: 250°F
Try these wood chips: Cherry, hickory or mesquite

Ingredients:

Flatbreads	Dressing
❑ 4 pcs. prepared flatbread	❑ ½ cup white barbecue sauce
❑ 8 oz. Perfectly Smoked Prime Rib	
❑ 1 cup mozzarella cheese, shredded	
❑ 1 cup baby arugula	
❑ 1 cup grape tomatoes, halved	

Preparation:
1. Preheat smoker to 275°F
2. Chop prime rib into small pieces, set aside.
3. Top each flatbread with cheese, prime rib, and grape tomatoes.
4. Place the flatbread directly onto the smoker grates and smoke 20-30 minutes or until the cheese is melted.
5. Remove from the smoker and top each flatbread with arugula and a drizzle of white barbecue sauce.
6. Cut into sections and serve immediately.

Note: These flatbread can be made on the grill by placing the flatbreads over medium heat with the lid down, or in a 400°F oven for 7-9 minutes.

PRIME RIB PIZZA

Serves: 4-6 | **Preparation Time:** 6-7 hours

If you have never experienced prime rib pizza, you don't know what you're missing. Adding a generous helping of chopped prime rib to an ordinary pizza gives it that upscale feeling you need while you binge watch the last season of that one show.

Estimated Smoke Time: 8-10 Hours (1 hour per lb.)
Smoke Temp: 250°F
Try these wood chips: Cherry, hickory or mesquite

Ingredients:

Pizza	Sauce
❏ 1 large prepared pizza crust, store-bought or homemade ❏ ½ lb. Perfectly Smoked Prime Rib, chopped ❏ 1 cup fresh mushrooms, thinly sliced ❏ 1 cup provolone cheese, shredded ❏ 1 green onion, sliced	❏ Your favorite barbecue sauce (We like the Quick Barbecue Sauce for this recipe.)

Preparation:

1. Preheat smoker to 275°F or the oven to 450°F.
2. Place the pizza crust on a greased pizza pan. Top with barbecue sauce, cheese, chopped brisket, green onion, and thinly sliced mushrooms.
3. Smoke at 275°F for 30-40 minutes or until the cheese is melted or bake at 450°F for 4-5 minutes.

Tip: To par-bake pizza crust, stretch the dough to the desired shape and size and bake on a greased pizza pan, on the lowest rack, at 400°F for 4-5 minutes. This will cook the pizza crust halfway, allowing it to be finished in a smoker.

PERFECTLY SMOKED BEEF RIBS

Serves: 4-6 | **Preparation Time:** 10 min

This basic smoked beef ribs recipe uses the 3-2-1 method of cooking. Once you understand the technique, you can customize the flavors according to your whim and fancy.

Estimated Smoke Time: 5 hours
Smoke Temp: 225°F
Try these wood chips: Cherry, hickory or mesquite

Ingredients:

Meat	Rub	Sauce
❑ 2 (3-4 lb.) racks beef back ribs	❑ 2 cups Basic Beef Rub	❑ ½ cup of your favorite barbecue sauce, we like the Classic Texas Barbecue Sauce for this preparation

Preparation:
1. Pat the ribs dry with a paper towel.
2. With the bone side up, removing the membrane from the under-side of the beef ribs. This membrane is inedible and makes the beef ribs tough.
3. Liberally season both sides of the ribs with the Basic Beef Rub.
4. Let it sit for 30 minutes at room temperature while preheating the smoker to 225°F.

Smoking:
1. Set the ribs on the smoker grate, rib side down.
2. Smoke the ribs for 3 hours.
3. Remove the ribs and wrap them in aluminum foil with 2 Tbsp of beer or apple juice in the foil.
4. Return the ribs to the smoker for an additional 2 hours.
5. Remove the wrapped ribs, unwrap them completely and discard the aluminum foil.
6. Generously slather the smoked ribs with your favorite sauce.
7. Return the ribs to the smoker for 1 hour or until the sauce caramelizes and the internal temperature reaches 185°F.
8. Allow the ribs to rest 15 minutes before carving and serving.

LIP-SMACKIN' SHORT RIBS

Serves: 6 | **Preparation Time:** 1 hour, 10 min

Beef short ribs are considerably meatier than their back rib cousins. With lots of marbled fat and plenty of connective tissue, bone-in beef short ribs are ideal for the smoker. They are typically not sold as a rack, making even easier to cook.

Estimated Smoke Time: 5 hours
Smoke Temp: 225°F
Try these wood chips: Pecan, hickory or oak

Ingredients:

Meat	Rub
❑ 6 lbs bone-in short ribs	❑ ¼ cup Basic Beef Rub ❑ ¼ cup Worcestershire sauce

Preparation:
1. Rinse the ribs and pat them dry with a paper towel.
2. Trim any excess fat.
3. Brush the ribs with the Worcestershire sauce.
4. Coat the brushed ribs with the Basic Beef Rub.
5. Refrigerate the ribs for at least 1 hour.
6. After chilling, remove from the fridge and let it sit at room temperature for at least 30 minutes while preheating the smoker to 225°F.

Smoking:
1. Set the ribs directly on the smoker grate, meat side up.
2. Use the water pan for extra moist ribs.
3. Smoke the ribs for 5 hours or until the internal temperature reaches 185°F.
4. Let it sit for a 15 minutes before serving.

TIP: If you would like to sauce your beef short ribs, do so at the 3 hour mark to ensure the sauce has a chance to caramelize on the ribs.

"QUICK" SHORT RIB OSSO BUCCO

Serves: 6 | Preparation Time: 40 min

While it is unlikely you will have any short ribs left, making a few extras for this dish is completely worth it. Serve this dish over creamy polenta or mashed potatoes for a hearty, satisfying meal without the hassle.

Ingredients:

Meat	Other Ingredients
❏ 1 lb smoked short rib meat, shredded	❏ 2 cups beef stock
	❏ 1 cup red wine
	❏ 1 small onion, finely diced
	❏ 1 carrot, diced
	❏ 1 stalk celery, diced
	❏ 2 cloves garlic, mashed
	❏ 3 Tbsp extra-virgin olive oil
	❏ 3 Tbsp flour
	❏ 1 Tbsp tomato paste
	❏ 3 sprigs fresh thyme (1 tsp dried)
	❏ 1 stalk rosemary (1 tsp dried)
	❏ 1 orange

Preparation:

1. In a large, heavy bottomed Dutch oven, heat olive oil over medium heat.
2. Add onion, carrot, celery and garlic along with ½ tsp salt and ¼ tsp pepper and cook until soft, about 8 minutes.
3. Add tomato paste and flour and cook until tomato paste turns dark red.
4. Add wine and cook for 3 minutes or until mixture begins to thicken.
5. Add beef stock, rosemary, and thyme. Cook until mixture thickens slightly.
6. Add short rib meat and simmer, uncovered, for 20 minutes.
7. Serve over creamy polenta, mashed potatoes, or pasta.

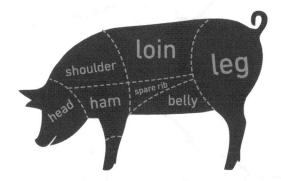

Pork

PERFECTLY SMOKED PORK BUTT

Pulled Pork Sandwich
Barbecue Apricot Summer Rolls
Hungarian Pulled Pork Sandwich
Southern-Style Barbecue Chili
Pulled Pork Tostadas
Pulled Pork Nachos
Kickin' Korean Lettuce Wraps

PERFECTLY SMOKED RIBS

Perfectly Smoked Spare Ribs
Perfectly Smoked Baby Back Ribs
World's Most Tender "3-2-1" Ribs
Smoked Asian Ribs
Country Style Pork Ribs

PERFECTLY SMOKED PORK LOIN

Fiery Pork Loin With Blueberry Chutney
Cuban Style Pork Loin
Cubano Sandwiches

PERFECTLY SMOKED PORK TENDERLOIN

Bourbon-Brown Sugar Pork Tenderloin
Pork Tenderloin Lettuce Wraps

SMOKED LOIN CHOPS

Chimichurri Smoked Loin Chops
Smoked Loin Chops With Cherry
   Chutney

PERFECTLY SMOKED BACON

Bacon Candy

PERFECTLY SMOKED PORK BUTT

Serves: 8-10 | **Preparation Time:** Active - 10 minutes; Passive - Overnight

This cut is the perfect place to start for beginner smokers. It always turns out great and it does not require any special technique to smoke it. This is a basic method, but we encourage you to experiment with the Texas Crutch to see if you like your bark a little softer.

Estimated Smoke Time: 8-16 hours
Smoke Temp: 225°F
Try these wood chips: Maple or fruitwood

Ingredients:

Meat	Rub
❏ 8-10 lbs. pork shoulder roast, preferably Boston Butt roast	❏ 2 cups Basic Barbecue Rub

Preparation:
1. Dry the pork butt with a paper towel.
2. Liberally apply the Basic Barbecue Rub to all surfaces of the meat.
3. Refrigerate the roast for 4-6 hours or overnight.
4. After chilling, remove the roast from the fridge and let it sit at room temperature for 30 minutes while preheating the smoker to 225°F.

Smoking:
1. Set the roast directly on the smoker grate.
2. Use the water pan for extra moist roast.
3. Smoke the roast until the internal temperature reaches 200°F.
4. Remove the roast from the smoker and allow it to rest for 30 minutes before handling. Using two forks, shred the meat and serve with your favorite barbecue sauce.

To use the Texas Crutch:
1. Smoke the roast for 4-6 hours, or until the internal temperature of the roast reads 150°F.
2. Remove the roast from the smoker.
3. Wrap the roast tightly in a double layer of heavy-duty aluminum foil with a splash of apple juice or beer inside the foil.
4. Return the roast back to smoker.
5. Remove the roast from the smoker once the internal temperature of the meat reaches 200°F.
6. Unwrap the roast and allow it to sit for 30 minutes until it is cool enough to handle.
7. Gently use two forks to shred the meat. Serve with preferred barbecue sauce.

PULLED PORK SANDWICH

Serves: 1 | Preparation Time: 5 min

This easy sandwich recipe is a sensational mix of meaty and tangy that hails from the South. Memphis slaw is a traditional coleslaw with a bell pepper kick, the perfect complement to the rich pork.

Ingredients:

Meat	Memphis Slaw	Other
❏ Perfectly Smoked Pork Butt, chopped	❏ 3 Tbsp red onions, grated ❏ 2 carrots, peeled and grated ❏ 1 medium green cabbage, shredded ❏ 1 green bell pepper, seeded, stemmed, and finely diced ❏ 2 cups mayonnaise ❏ ¾ cup sugar ❏ ¼ cup cider vinegar ❏ ¼ cup Dijon mustard ❏ 1 tsp salt ❏ 1 tsp Worcestershire sauce, optional ❏ ⬚ tsp black pepper, freshly ground	❏ Memphis slaw ❏ Texas toast ❏ preferred barbecue sauce

Preparation:

Memphis slaw
1. In a large bowl, mix together the cabbage, carrots, onion, and bell pepper. Toss well and set aside.
2. In another bowl, combine all the other ingredients.
3. Pour the second mixture over the cabbage mixture. Toss well until incorporated.
4. Cover the Memphis slaw and refrigerate for at least three hours.

Assembly:
1. Lay slices of the smoked pork butt meat onto the Texas toast.
2. Top with some Memphis slaw and drizzle with your preferred barbecue sauce.
3. Serve immediately.

BARBECUE APRICOT SUMMER ROLLS

Serves: 12-16 rolls | **Preparation Time:** 45 min

This recipe comes in handy if you're looking for a refreshing dish to serve for a summer barbecue. Mixing the spicy, savory flavors of Asia to the classic smoky taste of Southern barbecue is a fantastic fusion you don't want to miss.

Ingredients:

Meat	Peanut Sauce	Filling	Other
❑ 1 lb. Perfectly Smoked Pork Butt, chopped	❑ 4 tsp toasted sesame oil ❑ 3 Tbsp fresh lime juice ❑ 2 Tbsp soy sauce ❑ 2 tsp Asian hot chili sauce or Sriracha ❑ 2 garlic cloves, minced ❑ 2 green onions, finely chopped ❑ 1 cup sweet pepper relish ❑ 1 Tbsp ginger, freshly grated ❑ ½ cup cocktail peanuts, finely chopped	❑ 1 ½ cup fresh apricots, halved ❑ 1 large firm-ripe avocado, thinly sliced ❑ 1 sweet apple, peeled and cut into thin strips ❑ 1 English cucumber, cut into thin strips ❑ ½ cup fresh cilantro, roughly chopped ❑ ½ cup fresh mint, roughly chopped ❑ ½ cup fresh basil, roughly chopped	❑ 12-16 (8 to 9-inch) round rice paper sheets ❑ 12-16 Bibb lettuce leaves ❑ hot water

Preparation:

Peanut Sauce
1. In a mixing bowl, combine all ingredients together.
2. Transfer the mixture in an airtight container and refrigerate until ready to use.

Rice Paper Sheets
1. In a large, shallow dish, pour some hot water about 1 inch from the bottom of the dish.
2. Dip each rice paper sheet into the water for about 15-20 seconds.
3. Remove from water and pat-dry with paper towels. Set aside.

Assembly:
1. On a flat surface, place each softened rice paper sheet.
2. Place 3-4 apricot slices in the center of the rice paper.
3. Next, place 1 lettuce leaf, 2 cucumber strips, 1 avocado slice, 3-4 apple strips, 1 ½ to 2 Tbsp herbs, and 3 Tbsp smoked pork butt.
4. Fold each side over filling and roll it up like a burrito.
5. Place the rolls on a serving platter, seam side down.
6. Repeat the same process for the remaining rice paper sheets.
7. Upon serving, serve the apricot rolls with some of the peanut sauce.

HUNGARIAN PULLED PORK SANDWICH

Serves: 15 | **Preparation Time:** 8 hours

Turn up the flavor on your ordinary pulled pork sandwich by infusing it with some worldly aromatics like Hungarian sweet paprika and Spanish smoked paprika. There is so much going on in this pulled pork sandwich, it would be impossible to do it justice with words. You'll just have to try it yourself.

Estimated Smoke Time: 8-10 hours
Smoke Temp: 225°F
Try these wood chips: Maple, Alder, Fruitwood

Ingredients:

Meat	Rub	Sauce	Other
❏ 4 ½ lbs. pork shoulder, bone-in, Boston-butt	❏ 1 Tbsp Spanish smoked paprika ❏ 1 tsp Hungarian sweet paprika ❏ 1 Tbsp light brown sugar, firmly packed ❏ 1 tsp onion powder ❏ 1 tsp salt ❏ 1 tsp black pepper, freshly ground ❏ 1 tsp dry mustard ❏ 1 tsp red pepper, ground	❏ 2 cups apple cider vinegar ❏ ¾ cup ketchup ❏ 2 Tbsp granulated sugar ❏ 1 Tbsp hot pepper sauce ❏ 1 tsp salt ❏ 1 tsp dried red pepper, crushed ❏ ½ tsp black pepper, freshly ground	❏ 15 hamburger buns ❏ 1 (16-oz.) pack shredded coleslaw mix

Preparation:

Meat
1. In a large bowl, combine all rub ingredients.
2. Coat the prepared rub onto the Boston-butt and place the meat in a separate large bowl.
3. Refrigerate the pork butt, covered, for at least 8 hours or overnight, for best results.
4. After chilling, remove the meat from the fridge and let it sit for 30 minutes at room temperature as the smoker preheats to 225°F.

Sauce
1. In a microwave-safe bowl, mix together all sauce ingredients except the coleslaw mix.
2. Microwave the mixture on high setting for 2-3 minutes until the sugar is completely dissolved. Set aside to cool.

Coleslaw
1. In a large bowl, mix together ½ cup of the cooled, prepared sauce and the coleslaw mix. Toss the mixture properly and set aside.

Smoking:
1. Set the pork butt directly on the smoker grate.
2. Smoke it for 8-10 hours or until the internal temperature reaches 200°F.
3. Let it sit for a 30 minutes before carving.

Assembly:
1. Using 2 forks, shred the meat. Discard the fat and bone.
2. In a large bowl, mix together 2 cups of the prepared sauce and the shredded pork. Toss well.
3. Lay the bottom halves of the hamburger buns in a tray or large serving platter.
4. Spoon 5-6 Tbsp of the meat and 1/3 cup of the coleslaw on each bun half.
5. Place the upper halves of the burger buns to finish off the burgers.
6. Serve them with additional sauce for dipping.

SOUTHERN-STYLE BARBECUE CHILI

Serves: 8 | **Preparation Time:** 35 min

Try a new chili recipe that combines the incredible flavor of smoked barbecue pork and the heartiness of chili. Some people call this crack during harsh winter days, but it is perfect all year-round.

Pork Butt Roast Recipes

Ingredients:

Chili	Toppings
❏ 2 Tbsp extra-virgin olive oil	❏ avocado, sliced
❏ 1 small onion, chopped	❏ green onion, sliced
❏ 1 green bell pepper, chopped	❏ jalapeno, sliced
❏ 1 jalapeno, finely diced (optional)	❏ tortilla chips
❏ 2 cloves garlic, mashed	❏ cheese, shredded
❏ 1 ½ lb. Perfectly Smoked Pork Butt, chopped	❏ sour cream
❏ 2 (14.5-oz.) cans diced tomatoes, with green pepper, celery, and onions	
❏ 2 (14.5-oz) cans pinto beans, rinsed and drained	
❏ 1 (8-oz.) can tomato sauce	
❏ ¼ cup Chile Rub	

Preparation:

1. In a large Dutch oven, heat olive oil over medium heat.
2. Add onion, bell pepper, garlic and jalapeno and cook until soft.
3. Using two forks, shred the smoked pork butt.
4. Add Chile Rub and allow it to cook until fragrant.
5. Add pork butt, tomatoes, tomato sauce and pinto beans and bring to a simmer.
6. Reduce the heat and continue to simmer 15-20 minutes.
7. Serve with your choice of toppings.

PULLED PORK TOSTADAS

Serves: 4 | **Preparation Time:** 15 min

Add a Mexican vibe to classic pulled pork with this tostadas recipe. The delicious mixture of spices, fresh salsa, creamy avocado, smoked pork, and crumbled queso fresco heaping over a crunchy tostada shells makes this an enticing dish to dig into.

Ingredients:

Tostadas	Spices	Garnish
❏ 8 tostada shells	❏ 1 tsp chili powder	❏ ½ tsp fresh cilantro, chopped
❏ 1 lb. Perfectly Smoked Pork Butt, chopped	❏ 1 tsp ground cumin	❏ 1 cup fresh salsa
❏ 1 (16-oz.) can refried beans		❏ 1 cup queso fresco, crumbled
		❏ 2 avocados, chopped and dressed with 1 tsp lime juice
		❏ 2 cups shredded cabbage

Preparation:

1. In a large skillet, heat pork butt on low with chili powder and cumin.
2. In a separate small saucepan, heat refried beans.
3. Top tostada shells with beans, pork butt, and any garnishes you wish, just be sure to pile on the queso. fresco!

PULLED PORK NACHOS

Serves: 4 | **Preparation Time:** 15 min

Use up leftover smoked pork butt with this easy and tasty recipe. The smoky, savory flavor of the leftover meat matches well with the rich, flavorful sauce. Adding some lime wedges on the side gives your guests an option to add some zesty zing to this dish.

Ingredients:

Meat	Spices	Sauces
❏ 2 cups smoked pork butt, chopped and warmed	❏ 2 jalapeno peppers, thinly sliced ❏ 1 cup fresh salsa ❏ 1 (12-oz.) container refrigerated queso, warmed ❏ ▢ cup tomatoes, chopped ❏ ▢ cup fresh cilantro, chopped ❏ ½ cup black olives, sliced ❏ ½ cup red onion, minced	❏ 4 lime wedges ❏ 2-3 cups tortilla chips ❏ ½ tsp fresh cilantro, chopped, for garnish

Preparation:

1. In a microwave, warm the smoked pork.
2. In a platter, place the tortilla chips in one slightly heaping pile.
3. Pour a generous amount of the chopped smoked pork and other toppings.
4. Upon serving, top with chopped fresh cilantro and add the lime wedges on the side.

KICKIN' KOREAN LETTUCE WRAPS

Serves: 18 wraps | **Preparation Time:** 30 min

Koreans are huge barbecue fanatics just like Americans are. They share a love for full-flavored meat with us, but in a totally different way -- and that's what makes this dish spectacular. Featuring Asian ingredients like gochujang (a hot red pepper paste), ginger, soy sauce, and rice wine vinegar, the combination of these flavors will jolt your palate back to life if you're getting tired of the same ol' barbecue sauce. And instead of being served on buns, they use lettuce leaves for a healthier and lighter experience.

Ingredients:

Meat	Zucchini Salad	Sauce	Other
❏ 1 lb. Perfectly Smoked Pork Butt, chopped	❏ 3 Tbsp rice wine vinegar ❏ 3 Tbsp canola oil ❏ 2 shallots, minced ❏ 2 Tbsp sugar ❏ 2 Tbsp fresh cilantro, chopped ❏ 1 tsp Dijon mustard ❏ 1 zucchini, sliced thinly ❏ ¼ tsp salt ❏ ¼ tsp black pepper, freshly ground	❏ ½ cup soy sauce ❏ ¼ cup rice wine vinegar ❏ 2 Tbsp dark sesame oil ❏ 2 Tbsp light brown sugar, firmly packed ❏ 2 Tbsp gochujang or Sriracha sauce ❏ 1 Tbsp ginger, freshly grated ❏ 1 garlic clove, pressed	❏ 18 cabbage leaves (napa or savoy) ❏ 1-2 Tbsp oil-roasted cocktail peanuts, chopped

Preparation:

Zucchini Salad
1. In a large bowl, mix together the vinegar, Dijon mustard, sugar, salt, and pepper.
2. Slowly pour in the canola oil, a little at a time, whisking continuously until well-combined.
3. Toss in the zucchini slices, shallots, and cilantro until well incorporated.
4. Refrigerate for 15 minutes, covered.

Sauce
1. In a blender or food processor, mix all sauce ingredients until smooth. Set aside.

Assembly:
1. Lay the cabbage leave onto a tray or sheet pan.
2. Scoop about ¼ cup of the pork meat into each cabbage leaf.
3. Drizzle 1-2 Tbsp of the prepared sauce.
4. Scoop about 1-2 Tbsp of the chilled zucchini salad.
5. Finish off with a sprinkle of chopped cocktail peanuts. Serve immediately.

PERFECTLY SMOKED PORK SPARE RIBS

Serves: 8-10 | Preparation Time: Active -10 min; Passive - Overnight

Many smokers choose pork spare ribs or "St. Louis style spare ribs" over baby back ribs because they are generally meatier and more affordable. Be sure to brush the ribs with a light-colored oil as extra-virgin olive oil may burn.

Estimated Smoke Time: 5-6 hours
Smoke Temp: 225°F
Try these wood chips: Pecan, hickory, or cherry

Ingredients:

Meat	Rub	Other
❏ 3 (4-5 lb.) racks pork spareribs, St. Louis style, trimmed	❏ 2 cups Basic Barbecue Rub, or another rub of your choice ❏ ¼ cup peanut oil	❏ 2 cups favorite barbecue sauce (We like the Kansas City Style Barbecue Sauce.) ❏ 2 Tbsp apple juice, for spraying

Preparation:
1. Rinse the ribs and pat-dry with a paper towel.
2. Rub or brush the spareribs with a the peanut oil.
3. Next, rub the ribs with the Basic Barbecue Rub. Refrigerate overnight.
4. Preheat the smoker to 225°F.
5. Allow the ribs to come to room temperature for 30 minutes before smoking.

Smoking:
1. Set the ribs directly on the smoker grate, bone side down.
2. Use the water pan for extra moist ribs.
3. Smoke the ribs for 3 hours.
4. Remove the ribs from the smoker and spritz with a generous amount of apple juice.
5. Wrap them tightly in a double layer of heavy-duty aluminum foil.
6. Return them to the smoker, meat side down, and smoke for another 2 hours.
7. After 2 hours, remove them from the smoker and uncover. Discard the liquid together with the foil.
8. Brush 1-2 coats of your preferred barbecue sauce onto the ribs.
9. Smoke the ribs for another 45 minutes - 1 hour or until the sauce is set and the ribs reach an internal temperature of 185°F
10. Once done, remove from the smoker and let them rest for 10-15 minutes before carving. When serving, cut in-between bone to separate the ribs and serve with the remaining barbecue sauce.

PERFECTLY SMOKED BABY BACK RIBS

Serves: 8-10 | **Preparation Time:** 1 hour, 25 min

Smoking baby back ribs can be a little tricky as they tend to get overcooked quickly, but using your meat thermometer will ensure you wind up with perfect baby back ribs.

Estimated Smoke Time: 4-5 hours
Smoke Temp: 225°F
Try these wood chips: Pecan, hickory, or cherry

Ingredients:

Meat	Rub	Other
❑ 3 (3 lb.) slabs pork baby back ribs, trimmed	❑ 2 cups Basic Barbecue Rub ❑ ¼ cup peanut oil	❑ 2 cups of your favorite barbecue sauce ❑ 1/3 cup apple juice

Preparation:

Meat
1. Rinse the ribs and pat-dry with a paper towel.
2. Generously brush the ribs with peanut oil.
3. Next, rub the ribs with the Basic Barbecue Rub. Cover and refrigerate overnight.
4. Preheat the smoker to 225°F.
5. Allow the ribs to come to room temperature for 30 minutes before smoking.

Smoking:
1. Set the ribs directly on the smoker grate, bone side down.
2. Use the water pan for extra moist ribs.
3. Smoke the ribs for 1 ½ hours. Check occasionally to prevent the edges from getting charred.
4. Remove the ribs from the smoker and set each rack, meat side down, in each foil packet.
5. Wrap the ribs tightly with 2 Tbs apple juice in each foil packet and return to the smoker. Smoke for another 2 hours hours, still bone side down.
6. After 2 hours, remove them from the smoker and uncover. Discard the liquid together with the foil.
7. Brush 1-2 coats of the barbecue sauce onto the ribs.
8. Smoke the ribs for another 30-45 min, or until the sauce is set and the internal temperature reaches 185°F.
9. Once done, remove from the smoker and let them rest for 10-15 minutes before carving.
10. Upon serving, cut in-between bone to separate the ribs and serve with the remaining barbecue sauce.

WORLD'S MOST TENDER "3-2-1 RIBS"

Serves: 6 | **Preparation Time:** 15-25 min

The technique used in this recipe has many names -- the Texas crutch, 3-2-1 ribs, the aluminum foil method. Whatever you call it, smoking the ribs partially covered and then uncovered is a super easy way to achieve the coveted "fall off the bone" texture that meatheads crave.

Estimated Smoke Time: 6 hours
Smoke Temp: 225°F
Try these wood chips: Pecan or hickory, or mix of both

Ingredients:

Meat	Rub	Other
❏ 2 (~4 lb.) racks pork spare ribs, trimmed	❏ 1/3 cup Big Bold Barbecue Rub ❏ ¼ cup yellow mustard	❏ ½ cup apple juice

Preparation:

Meat
1. Rinse the spare ribs under cold water and pat-dry with a paper towel.
2. Put them on a cutting board, bone side up.
3. Coat both sides of the ribs with the mustard, and then sprinkle evenly with the rub.
4. Let it sit at room temperature while preheating the smoker to 225°F.

Smoking:
1. Set the ribs directly on the smoker grate, bone side down.
2. Smoke the ribs for 3 hours.
3. Remove the ribs from the smoker and set each rack in its own large piece of heavy-duty aluminum foil.
4. Pour ½ cup of the apple juice in each rack and immediately close the foil tightly around the ribs.
5. Return back to the smoker and smoke for another 2 hours.
6. After 2 hours, remove the ribs from the smoker and discard the foil.
7. Place them back to the smoker, directly on the smoker grate, and smoke for another hour.
8. Once done, remove from the smoker and allow to rest for 5-10 minutes before carving.

Note: Smoking the ribs directly on the smoker grate for another hour after smoking them with foil ensures that the ribs will have a crispy outer layer while the meat on the inside is tender enough to "fall right off the bone."

SMOKED ASIAN RIBS

Serves: 6 | **Preparation Time:** 15-25 min

Using seasoning and sauces that showcase the flavors and sensations from around the world is a delightful way to keep your barbecue fresh. This recipe also uses the 3-2-1 smoking method for extremely tender meat. Don't sweat it if you don't have all the ingredients you need -- great food is about experimenting and adapting, so make use of what you do have and substitute the rest with ingredients you think will serve the recipe well.

Estimated Smoke Time: 6 hours
Smoke Temp: 225°F
Try these wood chips: Pecan or fruitwood, or a mix of both

Ingredients:

Meat	Rub	Other
❏ 2 (~4 lb.) racks pork spare ribs	❏ 1/3 cup Asian Rub ❏ 3 Tbsp low-sodium soy sauce	❏ 1 cup Chinese Barbecue Sauce ❏ ½ cup apple juice

Preparation:

Meat
1. Rinse the spare ribs under cold water and pat-dry with a paper towel.
2. Put them on a cutting board, bone side up.
3. Remove the membrane and the flap of meat running along the entire length of the ribs.
4. After trimming, thinly coat both sides of the ribs with soy sauce, and then, sprinkle evenly with the rub.
5. Let it sit at room temperature while preheating the smoker to 225°F.

Smoking:
1. Set the ribs directly on the smoker grate, bone side down.
2. Smoke the ribs for 3 hours.
3. Remove the ribs from the smoker and set each rack on a heavy-duty aluminum foil.
4. Pour ¼ cup of the apple juice in each rack and immediately close the foil tightly around the ribs.
5. Return back to the smoker and smoke for another 2 hours.
6. After 2 hours, remove the ribs from the smoker and from the foil.
7. Brush the ribs with Chinese Barbecue Sauce and place them back on the smoker grates. Smoke for another hour, or until the internal temperature reaches 185°F.
8. Once done, remove from the smoker and allow to cool for 15 minutes before carving.
9. Serve with more Chinese Barbecue Sauce on the side.

COUNTRY STYLE PORK RIBS

Serves: 4 | **Preparation Time:** 25 min

Truly delicious barbecue that is super tender and moist is a labor of love. Country style ribs are great because they are boneless rib-like strips of meat that are budget friendly -- and they're not actually from the ribs, but the shoulder region. Paired with a special barbecue sauce, this recipe is "heaven on earth", great for a happy dinner with the family.

Estimated Smoke Time: 3-4 hours
Smoke Temp: 240°F
Try these wood chips: Cherry

Ingredients:

Meat	Rub	Sauce
❏ 2 lbs. meat strips	❏ ¼ cup Cajun Dry Rub	❏ 2 cups of your favorite barbecue sauce (We love the Quick Barbecue Sauce for an easy weeknight meal.)

Preparation:

Meat
1. Rinse the meat strips under cold water and pat-dry with a paper towel.
2. Sprinkle the strips with the Cajun Dry Rub. Set aside.
3. Let it sit at room temperature while preheating the smoker to 240°F.

Smoking:
1. Set the strips directly on the smoker grate.
2. Smoke the strips for 1 hour.
3. Remove them from the smoker and set the strips on an aluminum pan.
4. Pour the barbecue sauce over the strips and cover them with a heavy-duty aluminum foil.
5. Return back to the smoker and smoke for another 2-3 hours or until the internal temperature reaches 185°F.
6. Serve with more barbecue sauce on the side.

PERFECTLY SMOKED PORK LOIN

Serves: 8-10 | Preparation Time: 35 min

Pork Loin should never be treated like pork shoulder on the smoker. Instead, think of it like a beef tenderloin - at its most juicy and flavorful when it is cooked to a perfect medium. With modern breeding practices, cooking pork until it is well done is no longer necessary. However, if you still prefer your pork loin a little more on the "done" side, pull it out of the smoker at 155°F and cover it with aluminum foil. The heat from the meat will carry the internal temperature to 160°F, or just cooked through.

Estimated Smoke Time: 2 ½-3 hours
Smoke Temp: 250°F
Try these wood chips: Cherry or other fruit wood

Ingredients:

Meat	Rub
❑ 1 (3-4 lb.) boneless pork loin	❑ 3 Tbsp Grill Seasoning ❑ 2 Tbsp whole-grain mustard

Preparation:

Meat
1. Rinse the pork loin and pat-dry with a paper towel.
2. Spread the loin with the whole-grain mustard and sprinkle with grill seasoning.
3. Let it sit at room temperature while preheating the smoker to 250°F.

Smoking:
1. Set the loin directly on the smoker grate.
2. Smoke the loin for 2 hours.
3. Insert a meat thermometer at the thickest portion of the meat halfway before the smoking time is done.
4. Remove the loin from the smoker once the internal temperature reaches 145°F.
5. Cover the loin with aluminum foil and allow the meat to rest for 20-25 minutes before carving.
6. Upon serving, slice the loin into ½ inch slices and serve.

FIERY PORK LOIN WITH BLUEBERRY CHUTNEY

Serves: 8-10 | **Preparation Time:** 35 min

The meaty flavor of the pork loin is perfectly accented by the sweet and spicy chutney. This dish is perfect for those late spring days when the blueberries are ripe and the warm temperatures lure you outside.

Estimated Smoke Time: 2 ½-3 hours
Smoke Temp: 250°F
Try these wood chips: Cherry

Ingredients:

Meat	Rub	Blueberry Chutney
❑ 1 (3-4 lb.) boneless pork loin	❑ 3 Tbsp Grill Seasoning ❑ 2 Tbsp whole-grain mustard	❑ 2 Tbsp red wine vinegar ❑ 2 jalapenos, seeded and finely diced ❑ 2 garlic cloves, minced ❑ 1 Tbsp olive oil ❑ 1 medium red onion, finely chopped ❑ 1 lb. fresh blueberries ❑ 1/3 cup sugar

Preparation:

Meat
1. Rinse the pork loin and pat-dry with a paper towel.
2. Spread the loin with the whole-grain mustard and sprinkle with grill seasoning.
3. Let it sit at room temperature while preheating the smoker to 250°F.

Blueberry Chutney
1. In a small saucepan, saute the onion, garlic, and ginger in olive oil over medium heat for 4-5 minutes or until the onion becomes translucent.
2. Stir in the blueberries and jalapeno and cook for another 4 minutes.
3. Pour the vinegar and add in the sugar, bring to a boil.
4. Once boiling, reduce the heat and let the mixture simmer for 8-10 minutes, stirring from time to time.
5. Remove from heat and set aside.

Smoking:
1. Set the loin directly on the smoker grate.
2. Smoke the loin for 2 hours or until the loin reaches an internal temperature of 145°F.
3. Cover the loin with aluminum foil and allow the meat to rest for 20-25 minutes before carving.
4. Upon serving, slice the loin into ½ inch slices and top each with a spoonful of blueberry chutney. Serve.

CUBAN STYLE PORK LOIN

Serves: 8-10 | **Preparation Time:** Active - 10 min; Passive - 4 hours-Overnight

Cubans love pork. It is common to ride through the streets of Miami on New Year's Eve and smell porky goodness in the air as families roast whole pigs in wooden boxes called a "Caja Chinas". Typically marinated in sour orange juice, garlic, and cumin, Cuban "lechon asado" is highly addictive. Since sour oranges aren't typically found outside of South Florida, a combination of orange juice and lime juice does the trick.

Estimated Smoke Time: 2 ½-3 hours
Smoke Temp: 250°F
Try these wood chips: Cherry or other fruit wood

Ingredients:

Meat	Marinade
❏ 1 (3-4 lb.) boneless pork loin	❏ 8 cloves garlic, minced ❏ 1 cup freshly squeezed orange juice ❏ ½ cup freshly squeezed lime juice ❏ 2 tsp cumin ❏ 1 tsp salt ❏ ½ tsp black pepper

Preparation:

Meat
1. Rinse the pork loin and pat-dry with a paper towel.
2. In a large zip-top bag, combine marinade ingredients.
3. Place pork loin in the zip top bag and refrigerate 4 hours or overnight.
4. Remove the roast from the marinade and allow it to come to room temperature for 30 minutes while preheating the smoker to 250°F.
5. Place the leftover marinade in a small sauce pan and simmer over medium heat until it has reduced by half. Set aside.

Smoking:
1. Set the loin directly on the smoker grate.
2. Smoke the loin for 2 hours or until the internal temperature reaches 135°F.
3. Remove the loin from the smoker and brush with the reduced marinade. Return to the smoker and cook until the loin reaches 145°F.
4. Cover the loin with aluminum foil and allow the meat to rest for 20-25 minutes before carving.

CUBANO SANDWICHES

Serves: 6 | **Preparation Time:** 20 min

Also known as "medianoches", these sandwiches are meant to be eaten at midnight, once the large meal is over and the dancing has begun.

Ingredients:

Meat	Marinade
❏ 1 lb. boneless pork loin, thinly sliced	❏ 6 hoagie rolls or other crusty roll
❏ 1 lb thinly sliced deli ham	❏ ½ lb swiss cheese
	❏ Dill pickle slices
	❏ ¼ cup (½ stick) melted butter
	❏ ¼ c yellow mustard

Preparation:
1. Slice each hoagie roll lengthwise and lay open.
2. Spread one side with yellow mustard
3. Layer sliced pork loin, ham, Swiss cheese, and dill pickle slices on one side of the bread.
4. Close the sandwich and brush the top and bottom with melted butter.
5. Place sandwiches in a panini press and cook until brown and crispy on the outside and warm and gooey on the inside.

TIP: If you do not have a panini press, heat a skillet over medium. Place sandwiches in the skillet then top with a second skillet, weighted down by 2-3 cans of vegetables.

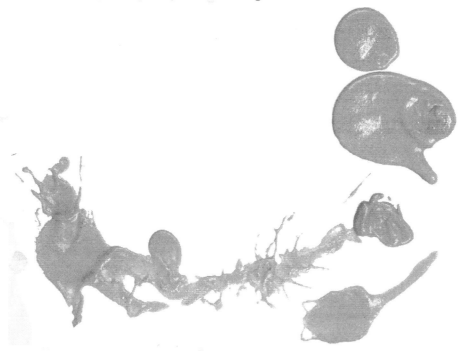

PERFECTLY SMOKED PORK TENDERLOIN

Serves: 6 | **Preparation Time:** 30 min

Like its beef counterpart, pork tenderloin is prized for its texture, but not necessarily for its flavor. The challenge then becomes infusing as much flavor into the meat as possible, without compromising the texture. This basic recipe does the trick as mustard helps create the delicious barbecue crust you often lack with tenderloin.

Estimated Smoke Time: 1 ½ - 2 hours
Smoke Temp: 225°F
Try these wood chips: Cherry or other fruit wood

Ingredients:

Meat	Rub
❏ 2 pork tenderloins	❏ Big Bold Barbecue Rub ❏ ¼ cup whole grain mustard

Preparation:
1. Trim any silverskin or excess fat from the tenderloins and pat them dry.
2. Cut off the smaller ends to allow the tenderloins to cook more evenly. These smaller pieces will cook more quickly and smoking them separately allows them to be removed when they are finished.
3. Brush the tenderloins on all sides with whole grain mustard and season liberally with Big Bold Barbecue Rub.
4. Set aside while the smoker comes to 225°F.

Smoking:
1. Place the tenderloins directly on the smoker grates.
2. Cook until they reach an internal temperature of 145°F.
3. Remove tenderloins from the smoker and allow them to rest for 15-20 minutes before carving.

BOURBON-BROWN SUGAR PORK TENDERLOIN

Serves: 6-8 | **Preparation Time:** 15 min

This sweet and savory rub combined with a bourbon-laced barbecue sauce gives this pork tenderloin exactly what it needs.

Estimated Smoke Time: 1 ½ - 2 hours
Smoke Temp: 225°F
Try these wood chips: Cherry or other fruit wood

Ingredients:

Meat	Rub	Sauce
❏ 2 Pork Tenderloins	❏ Classic American Brown Sugar Dry Rub ❏ ¼ cup Real Maple Syrup	❏ Memphis Barbecue Sauce

Preparation:
1. Rinse and pat the pork tenderloins dry. Trim off smaller end pieces.
2. Brush tenderloins with real maple syrup and liberally apply the Classic American Brown Sugar Dry Rub.
3. Set aside while the smoker preheats to 225°F.

Smoking:
1. Place the tenderloins directly on the smoker grates.
2. Smoke until the internal temperature reaches 130°F.
3. Remove the tenderloins from the smoker and brush liberally with the Memphis Barbecue Sauce.
4. Return the tenderloins to the smoker and continue cooking until they reach an internal temperature of 145°F.
5. Remove them from the smoker and allow them to rest for 10-15 minutes before carving.

PORK TENDERLOIN LETTUCE WRAPS

Serves: 6-8 | **Preparation Time:** 45 min

Loosely based on Korean "bulgogi", these pork tenderloin lettuce wraps are the perfect sweet and spicy mouthful on a hot summer day.

Estimated Smoke Time: 1 ½ - 2 hours
Smoke Temp: 225°F
Try these wood chips: Cherry or other fruit wood

Ingredients:

Meat	Marinade	Other
❏ 2 Pork Tenderloins	❏ 4 large garlic cloves ❏ 2 Tbsp sriracha or sambal ❏ 1 cup peeled, chopped ripe pear ❏ ¾ cup finely chopped onion ❏ 1 tsp finely chopped ginger ❏ 1 scallion, chopped ❏ 2 Tbsp soy sauce ❏ 1 Tbsp sesame oil ❏ 1 Tbsp light brown sugar or honey ❏ ½ tsp black pepper	❏ 2 cups cooked rice ❏ 2 scallions, thinly sliced ❏ 1 head, bib lettuce ❏ 1 cucumber, julienned ❏ 1 carrot, julienned ❏ ½ cup Chinese Barbecue Sauce

Preparation:
1. In a food processor, combine all marinade ingredients and process until smooth.
2. Rinse and pat the pork tenderloins dry. Trim off smaller end pieces.
3. Place tenderloins in a zip top bag with the marinade and allow to sit for a minimum of 30 minutes. This can also be done the night before since the longer the tenderloins marinate, the better.
4. Allow the tenderloins to come to room temperature while the smoker preheats to 225°F.

Smoking:
1. Place the tenderloins directly on the smoker grates.
2. Smoke until the internal temperature reaches 145°F.
3. Remove them from the smoker and allow them to rest for 10-15 minutes before carving.

Assembly:
1. Thinly slice the pork tenderloins.
2. Place pork, a small amount of rice, vegetables and a drizzle of sauce in a lettuce leaf.
3. Try not to look like a hog as you devour these one after another after another.

PERFECTLY SMOKED LOIN CHOPS

Serves: 6 | **Preparation Time:** Active - 10 minutes; Passive - 1 hour-Overnight

Loin chops are pieces of the pork loin, cut into smaller pieces. Because the chops don't have the benefit of being a part of a larger roast, they tend to dry out and overcook quickly. The best way to combat this is to purchase extra thick chops and brine them before smoking.

Estimated Smoke Time: 1 hour
Smoke Temp: 225°F
Try these wood chips: Fruit woods

Ingredients:

Meat	Brine
❑ 6 loin chops, cut 2 inches thick	❑ 4 cups crushed ice
	❑ ½ gallon hot water
	❑ ½ cup Kosher Salt
	❑ ½ cup brown sugar

Preparation:
1. In a large, non-reactive bowl, combine water, salt and sugar and stir until dissolved.
2. Add crushed ice to chill brine and pork chops when the ice has melted.
3. Allow to sit in the refrigerator for at least 1 hour and up to overnight.
4. Preheat the smoker to 225°F.
5. Remove the chops from the brine, pat dry and allow to sit at room temperature for 30 minutes before smoking.

Smoking:
1. Place the loin chops directly on the smoker grates.
2. Smoke the chops until the internal temperature reaches 145°F.
3. Remove the chops from the smoker and allow them to rest 10-15 minutes before serving.

CHIMICHURRI SMOKED LOIN CHOPS

Serves: 6 | **Preparation Time:** Active - 10 minutes; Passive - 1 hour-Overnight

Chimichurri is a garlicky, herby condiment popular in South American cuisine. The secret to this bold sauce is curly parsley. Who knew?

Estimated Smoke Time: 1 hour
Smoke Temp: 225°F
Try these wood chips: Fruit woods

Ingredients:

Meat	Brine	Chimichurri
❑ 6 loin chops, cut 2 inches thick	❑ 4 cups crushed ice	❑ 3 cloves garlic
	❑ 4 cloves garlic, whole	❑ 2 Tbsp red wine vinegar
	❑ 2 limes, halved	❑ 1 bunch curly parsley
	❑ ½ gallon hot water	❑ ¾ cup extra-virgin olive oil
	❑ ½ cup Kosher Salt	❑ 1 tsp red pepper flakes
	❑ ½ cup brown sugar	❑ ½ tsp Kosher salt

Preparation:
1. In a large, non-reactive bowl, combine water, salt and sugar and stir until dissolved.
2. Add crushed ice, limes, and garlic to the brine. Add pork chops when the ice has melted.
3. Allow to sit in the refrigerator for at least 1 hour and up to overnight.
4. Preheat the smoker to 225°F.
5. Remove the chops from the brine, pat dry and allow to sit at room temperature for 30 minutes before smoking.
6. In a food processor, pulse parsley, garlic, red pepper flake, and salt until chopped. Add vinegar.
7. With the food processor running, stream in the olive oil. This sauce gets better the longer it sits.

Smoking:
1. Place the loin chops directly on the smoker grates.
2. Smoke the chops until the internal temperature reaches 145°F.
3. Remove the chops from the smoker and allow them to rest 10-15 minutes before serving.
4. Spoon chimichurri over the pork chops when serving.

SMOKED LOIN CHOPS WITH CHERRY CHUTNEY

Serves: 6 | **Preparation Time:** Active - 10 minutes; Passive - 1 hour-Overnight

Pork and cherries go very well together. This cherry chutney is an especially delicious accompaniment to the smoky pork chops. You may want to make a double batch to spread on plain grilled chicken.

Estimated Smoke Time: 1 hour
Smoke Temp: 225°F
Try these wood chips: Fruit woods

Ingredients:

Meat	Brine	Cherry Chutney
❏ 6 loin chops, cut 2 inches thick	❏ 4 cups crushed ice ❏ ½ gallon hot water ❏ ½ cup Kosher Salt ❏ ½ cup brown sugar	❏ 2 cups fresh cherries, pitted (you can also use frozen that have been thawed) ❏ ¾ cup cherry preserves ❏ 2/3 cup chopped onion ❏ 3 Tbsp balsamic vinegar ❏ 1 Tbsp vegetable oil ❏ 1 tsp fresh thyme ❏ ½ tsp ground allspice ❏ ¼ tsp cayenne pepper

Preparation:

1. In a large, non-reactive bowl, combine water, salt and sugar and stir until dissolved.
2. Add crushed ice to the brine. Add pork chops when the ice has melted.
3. Allow to sit in the refrigerator for at least 1 hour and up to overnight.
4. Preheat the smoker to 225°F.
5. Remove the chops from the brine, pat dry and allow to sit at room temperature for 30 minutes before smoking.
6. In a medium saucepan, heat oil over medium heat. Add onion and saute for 8 minutes or until the onion is translucent.
7. Add allspice, cayenne, and thyme to the oil and onion and allow the spices to become fragrant, about 1 minute.
8. Add cherry preserves, balsamic vinegar, and fresh cherries. Stir and reduce the heat to low.
9. Allow the sauce to simmer 10 minutes, or until the chutney is thick.
10. Reserve ½ cup of the chutney for glazing and set the rest aside.

Smoking:

1. Place the loin chops directly on the smoker grates.
2. Smoke the chops until the internal temperature reaches 135°F.
3. Remove the chops from the smoker and brush liberally with the reserved chutney.
4. Return the chops to the smoker until the internal temperature reaches 145°F.
5. Remove the chops from the smoker and allow them to rest 10-15 minutes before serving.
6. Serve with the remaining chutney.

PERFECTLY SMOKED BACON

Serves: 3 lbs. of bacon | **Preparation Time:** 7 days

Why buy bacon when it's easy to make one your own? This restaurant-style smoked bacon recipe involves just a few ingredients and the rest of the magic comes from curing and smoking the meat. This particular recipe calls for a specialized ingredient called "Prague Powder #1", a curing salt that contains salt and sodium nitrate and is ideal for home curing meats. It is available at sporting good stores, butcher shops, and online retailers.

Estimated Smoke Time: 2 hours
Smoke Temp: 225°F
Try these wood chips: Pecan, cherry, apple, or hickory

Ingredients:

Meat	Cure
❏ 1 3-lb piece of fresh pork belly	❏ ¾ cup distilled water
	❏ 6 Tbsp dark brown sugar
	❏ 2 Tbsp kosher salt
	❏ 3 tsp black pepper
	❏ 1 ½ tsp Prague Powder #1

Preparation:

Meat
1. Rinse the pork belly and pat-dry with a paper towel.
2. In a large zip top bag, combine cure ingredients.
3. Submerge pork belly into the bag and close, placing the bag in a container in the refrigerator for 7 days, making sure to flip the bag over every day and massage the pork belly to redistribute the spices.
4. Remove the pork belly from the fridge and thoroughly wash it under cold water to stop the curing process.
5. Sprinkle the slab generously with freshly ground pepper, if you want pepper bacon.
6. Let it sit at room temperature while preheating the smoker to 225°F.

Smoking:
1. Set the pork belly directly on the smoker grate.
2. Smoke 2 hours or until the internal temperature reaches 165°F.
3. Remove the bacon from the smoker and allow to cool.
4. Wrap the bacon in plastic wrap and refrigerate overnight so the it will be firm enough to slice.
5. When you're ready to cook the bacon, slice and cook as you would with store-bought bacon.

Note: If you decide to store the bac on, place the unused pieces in wax paper and then wrap tightly with plastic wrap and freeze for up to 2 months.

BACON CANDY

Serves: 12 slices | **Preparation Time:** 1 hour, 25 min

This recipe has wonderful combination of sweetness, saltiness, and savoriness all rolled into one. Be warned, this dish is totally addictive! Serve whole for a tasty snack or break up into bits to serve as a topping for salads, vanilla ice cream, or pasta.

Estimated Smoke Time: 30 minutes
Smoke Temp: 275°F
Try these wood chips: Pecan, cherry, apple, or hickory

Ingredients:

Meat	Rub
❑ 12 slices of homemade Smoked Bacon	❑ 1 cup brown sugar, lightly packed ❑ ½ cup Basic Barbecue Rub

Preparation:
1. In a baking sheet, place a sheet of parchment paper.
2. Place the bacon slices across the baking sheet and sprinkle with a liberal amount of rub and brown sugar.
3. Let it sit at room temperature while preheating the smoker to 275°F.

Smoking:
1. Set the bacon slices directly on the smoker grate.
2. Smoke them for 30-45 minutes or until they become crispy and caramelized.
3. Remove them from the smoker and allow to cool before serving.

POULTRY

PERFECTLY SMOKED CHICKEN WINGS

Spicy Honey Apple Barbecue Wings
SmoFried (Smoked, then fried) Chicken
    Wings
Red Hot Chicken Wings

SMOKED WHOLE CHICKEN

Old-fashioned Barbecue Chicken
Grandma's Whole Smoked Chicken

SMOKED CHICKEN QUARTERS

Asian Chicken Quarters
Lemon Pepper Chicken Quarters
Maple Mustard Chicken Quarters

SMOKED CHICKEN BREASTS

Monterey Chicken
Cola Glazed Chicken Breasts

SMOKED WHOLE TURKEY

Smo-Fried Cajun Turkey

SMOKED TURKEY LEGS

Chipotle Turkey Legs
White Bean Soup With Smoked Turkey

GAME DAY CORNISH HENS

PERFECTLY SMOKED CHICKEN WINGS

Serves: 8 | **Preparation Time:** 45 min

Most chicken cooked in a smoker is in need of two things - a brine or marinade, and a secondary cooking method to crisp up the skin. It is nearly impossible to get crispy skin on wings from a smoker. By allowing the wings to spend just two minutes under the broiler in your home oven after smoking, you will wind up with firm, tasty skin.

Estimated Smoke Time: 1-1½ hours
Smoke Temp: 250°F
Try these wood chips: Pecan, cherry, apple, or hickory

Ingredients:

Meat	Brine	Sauce
❑ 5 lbs chicken wings	❑ 4 cups crushed ice ❑ ½ gallon hot water ❑ ½ cup Kosher salt ❑ ½ cup brown sugar	❑ 1 bottle Frank's Red Hot ❑ 1 cup (2 sticks) melted butter

Preparation:
1. In a large bowl, combine hot water, salt, and brown sugar and stir until dissolved. Add ice and chicken wings.
2. Allow the wings to brine in the refrigerator for a minimum of 30 minutes and up to 3 hours.
3. Remove the wings from the fridge and preheat the smoker to 250°F.

Smoking:
1. Set the wings slices directly on the smoker grate.
2. Smoke them for 1-1 ½ hours or until the internal temperature reaches 165°F.
3. Meanwhile, combine melted butter and hot sauce in a large bowl.
4. Remove wings from the smoker and toss in the sauce.
5. Place on foil-lined baking trays and finish under the broiler for 2 minutes, or until the skin becomes crispy.

SPICY HONEY-APPLE BBQ WINGS

Serves: 6 | **Preparation Time:** 1 hour - Overnight

Who wouldn't love spicy barbecue wings to get the party started? Ditch your regular buffalo wings in favor of this sweet and spicy alternative. You won't be disappointed.

Estimated Smoke Time: 1-1½ hours
Smoke Temp: 250°F
Try these wood chips: Pecan, cherry, apple, or hickory

Ingredients:

Meat	Rub	Sauce
❏ 5 lbs chicken wings	❏ ¼ cup Big Bold Barbecue Rub	❏ 2 cups Honey Chipotle Barbecue Sauce ❏ ¼ cup apple jam or apple butter

Preparation:
1. In a large zip top bag, combine chicken wings and rub.
2. Allow the wings to sit in the refrigerator for a minimum of 1 hour and up to overnight.
3. Remove the wings from the fridge and preheat the smoker to 250°F.

Smoking:
1. Set the wings slices directly on the smoker grate.
2. Smoke them for 1-1 ½ hours or until the internal temperature reaches 165°F.
3. Meanwhile, combine barbecue sauce and apple jam in a medium saucepan and warm on low for 10 minutes.
4. Remove wings from the smoker and toss in the sauce.
5. Place on foil-lined baking trays and finish under the broiler for 2 minutes, or until the skin becomes crispy.

SMOFRIED CHICKEN WINGS

Serves: 6-8 | **Preparation Time:** 1 hour

Another way to get crispy skin on smoked wings is to combine smoking and frying. While this may seem like an extra step that just isn't worth it, the crispy, smoky bites that emerge make up for the extra effort.

Estimated Smoke Time: 1-1 ½ hours
Smoke Temp: 250°F
Try these wood chips: Alder, pecan, or fruit woods

Ingredients:

Meat	Rub	Sauce
❏ 5 lbs chicken wings	❏ ¼ cup Money Rub	❏ 1 cup Chipotle Lime Mango Barbecue Sauce

Preparation:
1. In a large zip top bag, combine chicken wings and rub. Toss vigorously for a few minutes until all the pieces are evenly coated.
2. Let the chicken sit at room temperature while you preheat the smoker to 250°F.

Smoking:
1. Smoke the rubbed chicken wing pieces for until they reach an internal temperature of 165°F.
2. Meanwhile, heat ½ inch of oil in a large cast iron skillet until the oil reaches 375°F.
3. Fry the smoked wings in batches, in the hot oil for 45 seconds per side.
4. Set the fried wings over a paper towel to drain excess oil.
5. Toss in warmed sauce for an additional layer of flavor.

RED HOT CHICKEN WINGS

Serves: 6-8 | **Preparation Time:** 1 hour

Chileheads are almost as crazy about chiles as Meatheads are about barbecue. These wings are sure to please the spice lover in everyone.

Estimated Smoke Time: 1-1 ½ hours
Smoke Temp: 250°F
Try these Wood Chips: Pecan, mesquite

Ingredients:

Meat	Marinade	Rub
❑ 5 lbs chicken wings	❑ ½ cup your favorite hot sauce (we like sriracha)	❑ 2 Tbsp black pepper ❑ 2 tsp chili powder ❑ 2 tsp red pepper flakes ❑ 1 tsp onion powder ❑ 1 tsp garlic powder ❑ 1 tsp salt

Preparation:
1. In a large zip top bag, combine chicken wings and hot sauce. Let marinate in the fridge for 1 hour.
2. Mix together all rub ingredients in a large zip top bag.
3. Toss the chicken wings into the bag with the rub ingredients and shake the bag vigorously for a few minutes all the pieces are evenly coated.
4. Let the chicken sit at room temperature while you preheat the smoker to 250°F.

Smoking:
1. Smoke the rubbed chicken wing pieces for until they reach an internal temperature of 165°F.
2. Meanwhile, heat ½ inch of oil in a large cast iron skillet until the oil reaches 375°F.
3. Fry the smoked wings in batches, in the hot oil for 45 seconds per side.
4. Set the fried wings over a paper towel to drain excess oil.

WHOLE SMOKED CHICKEN

Serves: 4-6 | **Preparation Time:** 1 hour-Overnight

Estimated Smoke Time: 3-4 hours
Smoke Temp: 225°F
Try These Wood Chips: Alder, fruit woods

Ingredients:

Meat	Brine	Rub
❑ 1 3-4 lb roaster	❑ 1 gallon hot water ❑ 8 cups crushed ice ❑ 1 cup kosher salt ❑ 1 cup brown sugar ❑ 2 Tbsp whole peppercorns	❑ ¼ cup Money Rub

Preparation:
1. In a large non-reactive bowl, combine water, salt and sugar until salt and sugar are dissolved. Add peppercorns and crushed ice and stir to cool the brine.
2. Submerge the chicken in the brine and let sit in the fridge for 1 hour or as long as overnight.
3. When you are ready to smoke the bird, remove from the brine and dry with a paper towel.
4. Sprinkle the Money Rub on the skin and inside the cavity of the bird.
5. Let the chicken sit at room temperature while you preheat the smoker to 225°F.

Smoking:
1. Place the chicken, breast side down, in the smoker.
2. Smoke the chicken until the thigh meat reaches an internal temperature of 165°F.
3. Remove the chicken from the smoker and allow to sit, covered, for 15-20 minutes before carving.

OLD FASHIONED BARBECUE CHICKEN

Serves: 4-6 | **Preparation Time:** 1 hour-Overnight

There are a hundred different ways to prepare barbecue chicken. This same technique can be used with every rub and sauce combination you can think of.

Estimated Smoke Time: 3-4 hours
Smoke Temp: 225°F
Try These Wood Chips: Pecan, Mesquite

Ingredients:

Meat	Brine	Rub & Sauce
❏ 1 3-4 lb roaster	❏ 1 gallon hot water ❏ 8 cups crushed ice ❏ 1 cup kosher salt ❏ 1 cup brown sugar ❏ 2 Tbsp whole peppercorns	❏ ¼ cup Basic Barbecue Rub ❏ ¼ cup of your favorite barbecue sauce (We like the St. Louis Barbecue Sauce.)

Preparation:

1. In a large non-reactive bowl, combine water, salt and sugar until salt and sugar are dissolved. Add peppercorns and crushed ice and stir to cool the brine.
2. Submerge the chicken in the brine and let sit in the fridge for 1 hour or as long as overnight.
3. When you are ready to smoke the bird, remove from the brine and dry with a paper towel.
4. Sprinkle the Basic Barbecue Rub on the skin and inside the cavity of the bird.
5. Let the chicken sit at room temperature while you preheat the smoker to 225°F.

Smoking:

1. Place the chicken, breast side down, in the smoker.
2. Smoke the chicken until the thigh meat reaches an internal temperature of 155°F.
3. Remove the chicken from the smoker and brush liberally with barbecue sauce.
4. Return the chicken to the smoker until it reaches an internal temperature of 165°F.
5. Remove the chicken from the smoker and allow it to sit, lightly covered, for 15-20 minutes before carving.

GRANDMA'S WHOLE SMOKED CHICKEN

Serves: 4-6 | Preparation Time: 1 hour-Overnight

Just like grandma used to make -- but kicked up several notches. This recipe calls for brining a whole chicken -- and believe me, it is worth the extra effort if you love flavorful and juicy meat! It features a savory blend of Italian aromatics such as thyme and dried oregano mixed with desert heat from cayenne pepper.

Estimated Smoke Time: 3-4 hours
Smoke Temp: 225°F
Try These Wood Chips: Alder, fruit woods

Ingredients:

Meat	Brine	Rub
❏ 1 3-4 lb roaster	❏ 1 gallon hot water ❏ 8 cups crushed ice ❏ 1 cup kosher salt ❏ 1 cup brown sugar ❏ 1 tsp cayenne pepper	❏ ¼ cup extra-virgin olive oil ❏ ¼ cup soy sauce ❏ 1 Tbsp dried oregano ❏ 1 Tbsp dried thyme ❏ 2 tsp onion powder ❏ 2 tsp cayenne pepper ❏ 2 tsp paprika ❏ 2 tsp garlic powder or 2 crushed garlic cloves ❏ ½ - 1 tsp black pepper

Preparation:
1. In a large non-reactive bowl, combine water, salt and sugar until salt and sugar are dissolved. Add peppercorns and crushed ice and stir to cool the brine.
2. Submerge the chicken in the brine and let sit in the fridge for 1 hour or as long as overnight.
3. When you are ready to smoke the bird, remove from the brine and dry with a paper towel.
4. Combine the rub ingredients and rub into the skin, under the skin, and inside the cavity of the bird.
5. Let the chicken sit at room temperature while you preheat the smoker to 225°F.

Smoking:
1. Place the chicken, breast side down, in the smoker.
2. Smoke the chicken until the thigh meat reaches an internal temperature of 165°F.
3. Remove the chicken from the smoker and allow it to sit, lightly covered, for 15-20 minutes before carving.

SMOKED CHICKEN QUARTERS

Serves: 6 | **Preparation Time:** 1 hour-Overnight

When we talk about "chicken quarters" we are referring to legs and thighs, not breasts and wings. Dark meat has more flavor and retains moisture better than white meat, making it ideal for smoking.

Estimated Smoke Time: 1 ½ - 2 hours
Smoke Temp: 225°F
Try These Wood Chips: Pecan, fruit woods

Ingredients:

Meat	Brine	Rub
❑ 6 Chicken Quarters, dark meat only	❑ ½ gallon hot water ❑ 4 cups crushed ice ❑ ½ cup kosher salt ❑ ½ cup brown sugar ❑ 2 Tbsp whole peppercorns	❑ ¼ cup rub of your choice (We like the Mediterranean Spice Rub)

Preparation:
1. In a large non-reactive bowl, combine water, salt and sugar until salt and sugar are dissolved. Add peppercorns and crushed ice and stir to cool the brine.
2. Submerge the chicken in the brine and let sit in the fridge for 1 hour or as long as overnight.
3. When you are ready to smoke the bird, remove from the brine and dry with a paper towel.
4. Rub the Mediterranean Spice Rub into the skin, under the skin, and inside the cavity of the bird.
5. Let the chicken sit at room temperature while you preheat the smoker to 225°F.

Smoking:
1. Place the chicken directly on the grates of the smoker.
2. Smoke the chicken until the thigh meat reaches an internal temperature of 165°F.
3. Remove the chicken from the smoker and allow it to sit, lightly covered, for 15-20 minutes.

ASIAN CHICKEN QUARTERS

Serves: 6 | **Preparation Time:** 30 minutes

Make tasty, meaty chicken quarters even better with ginger, red pepper, brown sugar, and garlic. These are also great for smoking in large quantities.

Estimated Smoke Time: 1 ½ - 2 hours
Smoke Temp: 225°F
Try These Wood Chips: Pecan, fruit woods

Ingredients:

Meat	Rub	Sauce
❏ 6 Chicken Quarters, dark meat only	❏ 2 Tbsp peanut oil ❏ 1 Tbsp salt ❏ 1 Tbsp brown sugar ❏ 1 Tbsp cayenne pepper ❏ 1 tsp granulated garlic ❏ 1 tsp granulated onion ❏ 1 tsp ground ginger	❏ 1 cup Chinese Barbecue Sauce

Preparation:

1. In a mixing bowl, combine all rub ingredients and set aside.
2. Using your fingers, rub the mixture directly onto the chicken pieces.
3. Let the chicken sit at room temperature while you preheat the smoker to 225°F.

Smoking:

1. Once the smoker is ready, place each chicken piece directly onto the grate.
2. Smoke the chicken until the internal temperature reaches 155°F.
3. Remove the chicken from the smoker and brush with the Chinese Barbecue Sauce.
4. Return the chicken quarters to the smoker until they reach an internal temperature of 165°F.
5. Allow the chicken quarters to rest for 10-15 minutes before serving.

LEMON PEPPER CHICKEN QUARTERS

Serves: 6 | **Preparation Time:** 1 hour - Overnight

Zesty and zippy, these lemon pepper chicken quarters use lemon juice in the brine for an extra layer of flavor.

Estimated Smoke Time: 1 ½ - 2 hours
Smoke Temp: 225°F
Try These Wood Chips: Pecan, fruit woods

Ingredients:

Meat	Brine	Rub
❑ 6 Chicken Quarters, dark meat only	❑ ½ gallon hot water ❑ 4 cups crushed ice ❑ ½ cup Kosher salt ❑ ½ cup brown sugar ❑ 2 lemons, halved ❑ 2 Tbsp peppercorns	❑ ¼ cup Money Rub ❑ 2 Tbsp lemon zest ❑ 1 tsp black pepper

Preparation:
1. In a large non-reactive bowl, combine water, salt and sugar until salt and sugar are dissolved. Add peppercorns and crushed ice and squeeze lemons into the brine. Add squeezed lemons and stir to combine.
2. Submerge the chicken in the brine and let sit in the fridge for 1 hour or as long as overnight.
3. When you are ready to smoke the bird, remove from the brine and dry with a paper towel.
4. Mix black pepper, lemon zest and Money Rub and rub it into the skin, under the skin, and inside the cavity of the bird.
5. Let the chicken sit at room temperature while you preheat the smoker to 225°F.

Smoking:
1. Once the smoker is ready, place each chicken piece directly onto the grate.
2. Smoke the chicken until the internal temperature reaches 165°F.
3. Allow the chicken quarters to rest for 10-15 minutes before serving.

MAPLE MUSTARD CHICKEN QUARTERS

Serves: 6 | **Preparation Time:** 1 hour - Overnight

It sounds strange, but the combination of real maple syrup and Dijon mustard gives ordinary chicken quarters a sweet and spicy twist.

Estimated Smoke Time: 1 ½ - 2 hours
Smoke Temp: 225°F
Try These Wood Chips: Pecan, fruit woods

Ingredients:

Meat	Brine	Sauce
❏ 6 Chicken Quarters, dark meat only	❏ ½ gallon hot water ❏ 4 cups crushed ice ❏ ½ cup Kosher salt ❏ ½ cup brown sugar ❏ 2 Tbsp peppercorns	❏ ¼ cup real maple syrup ❏ ¼ cup Dijon mustard ❏ 3 cloves garlic, minced

Preparation:
1. In a large non-reactive bowl, combine water, salt and sugar until salt and sugar are dissolved. Add peppercorns and crushed ice and stir to combine.
2. Submerge the chicken in the brine and let sit in the fridge for 1 hour or as long as overnight.
3. Remove from the brine and dry with a paper towel.
4. Let the chicken sit at room temperature while you preheat the smoker to 225°F.

Smoking:
1. Once the smoker is ready, place each chicken piece directly onto the grate.
2. Smoke the chicken until the internal temperature reaches 150°F.
3. Combine sauce ingredients in a bowl and brush over the chicken pieces.
4. Return the chicken to the smoker and cook until the internal temperature reaches 165°F.
5. Allow the chicken quarters to rest for 10-15 minutes before serving.

SMOKED CHICKEN BREASTS

Serves: 4 | **Preparation Time:** Active - 10 minutes; Passive - 1 hour

Much like pork loin, smoking chicken breasts increases the likelihood of the meat drying out and becoming tough. Brining the chicken breasts, and cooking them with the bone in and skin on greatly reduces that risk.

Estimated Smoke Time: 45 minutes-1 hour
Smoke Temp: 250°F
Try these wood chips: Mesquite, Alder, Fruit wood

Ingredients:

Meat	Brine
❏ 4 bone in, skin on chicken breasts	❏ ½ gallon hot water ❏ 4 cups crushed ice ❏ ½ cup Kosher salt ❏ ½ cup brown sugar ❏ 2 Tbsp peppercorns ❏ 2 lemons, halved

Preparation:
1. In a large non-reactive bowl, combine water, salt and sugar until salt and sugar are dissolved. Add peppercorns, lemons, and crushed ice and stir to combine.
2. Submerge the chicken in the brine and let sit in the fridge for 1 hour.
3. Remove from the brine and dry with a paper towel.
4. Let the chicken sit at room temperature while you preheat the smoker to 250°F.

Smoking:
1. Once the smoker is ready, place each chicken piece directly onto the grate.
2. Smoke the chicken until the internal temperature reaches 165°F.
3. Allow the chicken breasts to rest for 10-15 minutes before serving.

MONTEREY CHICKEN

Serves: 4 | **Preparation Time:** Active - 10 minutes; Passive - 1 hour

Bacon. Chicken. Barbecue sauce. Pepper Jack Cheese. This might be nature's perfect food.

Estimated Smoke Time: 30-45 minutes
Smoke Temp: 250°F
Try these wood chips: Mesquite, Alder, Fruit wood

Ingredients:

Meat	Brine	Other
❏ 4 boneless, skinless chicken breasts	❏ 4 cups hot water ❏ 2 cups crushed ice ❏ ¼ cup Kosher salt ❏ ¼ cup brown sugar ❏ 1 Tbsp peppercorns ❏ 1 lemons, halved	❏ 8 thin strips of bacon ❏ 1 cup shredded pepper jack cheese ❏ ½ cup of your favorite barbecue sauce (We like our Kansas City Barbecue Sauce for this application) ❏ 2 Tbs Basic Barbecue Rub

Preparation:
1. In a large non-reactive bowl, combine water, salt and sugar until salt and sugar are dissolved. Add peppercorns, lemons, and crushed ice and stir to combine.
2. Submerge the chicken in the brine and let sit in the fridge for 1 hour.
3. Remove from the brine and dry with a paper towel.
4. Carefully wrap each chicken breast with the bacon, securing the ends with toothpicks. Sprinkle the bacon-covered chicken with Basic Barbecue Rub.
5. Let the chicken sit at room temperature while you preheat the smoker to 250°F.

Smoking:
1. Once the smoker is ready, place each chicken piece directly onto the grate.
2. Smoke the chicken until the internal temperature reaches 155°F.
3. Remove the chicken and baste with the barbecue sauce.
4. Return the chicken to the smoker until it reaches an internal temperature of 165°F.
5. Remove the chicken from the smoker and top with additional sauce and the pepper jack cheese.
6. Cover with aluminum foil and allow the chicken breasts to rest for 10-15 minutes, or until the cheese is melted.

COLA GLAZED CHICKEN BREASTS

Serves: 4 | **Preparation Time:** Active - 10 minutes; Passive - 1 hour

Cola products have been used for decades in barbecue sauces and marinades. Not only do they tenderize the meat, they provide a sweet, sticky glaze that leaves you licking your fingers.

Estimated Smoke Time: 45 minutes-1 hour
Smoke Temp: 250°F
Try these wood chips: Mesquite, Alder, Fruit wood

Ingredients:

Meat	Brine	Sauce
❏ 4 bone in, skin on chicken breasts	❏ ½ gallon hot water ❏ 4 cups crushed ice ❏ 1 cup cola ❏ ½ cup Kosher salt ❏ ½ cup brown sugar ❏ 2 Tbsp peppercorns	❏ 1 cup Cola Barbecue Sauce

Preparation:
1. In a large non-reactive bowl, combine water, salt and sugar until salt and sugar are dissolved. Add peppercorns, cola, and crushed ice and stir to combine.
2. Submerge the chicken in the brine and let sit in the fridge for 1 hour.
3. Remove from the brine and dry with a paper towel.
4. Let the chicken sit at room temperature while you preheat the smoker to 250°F.

Smoking:
1. Once the smoker is ready, place each chicken piece directly onto the grate.
2. Smoke the chicken until the internal temperature reaches 155°F.
3. Remove the chicken breasts from the smoker and liberally brush both sides with the Cola Barbecue Sauce.
4. Return the chicken breasts to the smoker and continue cooking until they reach an internal temperature of 165°F.
5. Allow the chicken to rest for 10-15 minutes before serving with additional heated sauce.

SMOKED WHOLE TURKEY

Serves: 10-12 | **Preparation Time:** Active - 10 minutes; Passive - 1 hour

Smoking a whole turkey is a long process, but one that yields a very flavorful bird. Brining the turkey and smoking it breast side down keeps the white meat moist and flavorful while the rest of the meat finishes cooking.

Estimated Smoke Time: 5-6 hours
Smoke Temp: 240°F
Try these wood chips: Mesquite, Alder, Fruit wood

Ingredients:

Meat	Brine
❏ 1 10-12-pound turkey, thawed with giblets removed	❏ 1 gallon hot water
	❏ 8 cups crushed ice
	❏ 5 garlic cloves, whole
	❏ 4 lemons, halved
	❏ 2 sprigs rosemary
	❏ 1 bundle fresh thyme
	❏ 1 cup Kosher salt
	❏ 1 cup brown sugar
	❏ ¼ cup peppercorns

Preparation:
1. In a large non-reactive bowl, combine water, salt and sugar until salt and sugar are dissolved. Add peppercorns, lemons, and crushed ice and stir to combine.
2. Submerge the turkey in the brine and let sit in the fridge for 1 hour.
3. Remove from the brine and dry with a paper towel.
4. Let the turkey sit at room temperature while you preheat the smoker to 240°F.

Smoking:
1. Once the smoker is ready, place the turkey directly onto the grate, breast side down.
2. Smoke the turkey until the internal temperature reaches 160°F when a thermometer is inserted in the deepest part of the thigh.
3. Remove the turkey from the smoker and cover with foil, allowing the bird to rest 20-30 minutes before carving.

SMO-FRIED CAJUN TURKEY

Serves: 10-12 | **Preparation Time:** Active - 10 minutes; Passive - 1 hour

Some people swear by fried turkey. They claim it is the fastest way to enjoy a tasty, juicy bird without all of the fuss of basting and brining. But fried turkey has a one-dimensional flavor that cannot be fixed with gravy alone. Enter smo-frying. By combining smoking and frying, turkeys remain moist and juicy, but still have a smoky, complex flavor. Adding Cajun seasoning to the brine takes things one step further as this turkey is one you will be talking about for years to come.

Estimated Smoke Time: 2 hours
Smoke Temp: 240°F
Try these wood chips: Mesquite, Alder, Fruit wood

Ingredients:

Meat	Brine	Other
❏ 1 10-12-pound turkey, thawed with giblets removed	❏ 1 gallon hot water ❏ 8 cups crushed ice ❏ 2 cups Cajun Dry Rub	❏ Turkey Frier ❏ 2-3 Gallons, Peanut Oil

Preparation:

1. In a large non-reactive bowl, combine water, Cajun Dry Rub, and crushed ice and stir to combine.
2. Submerge the turkey in the brine and let sit in the fridge for at least 1 hour.
3. Remove from the brine and dry with a paper towel.
4. Let the turkey sit at room temperature while you preheat the smoker to 240°F.

Smoking:

1. Once the smoker is ready, place the turkey directly onto the grate, breast side down.
2. Smoke the turkey for 2 hours.
3. Remove the turkey from the smoker and insert directly into a turkey frier, filled according to appliance directions, with 325°F peanut oil.
4. Continue to cook the turkey until the internal temperature of the meatiest part of the thigh reads 165°F.
5. Remove the bird from the oil, drain well, and allow the bird to rest 20-30 minutes before carving.

SMOKED TURKEY LEGS

Serves: 4 | **Preparation Time:** Active - 10 minutes; Passive - 1 hour

Have you ever been to a Renaissance Fair and watched as people walked around with giant turkey legs? There is something primal about carrying around a hunk of meat on a stick while you watch people joust. Even if you are only walking around your own backyard, tap into your ancestors from the middle ages and carry a smoked turkey leg with you.

Estimated Smoke Time: 4-5 hours
Smoke Temp: 250°F
Try these wood chips: Mesquite, Alder, Fruit wood

Ingredients:

Meat	Brine
❏ 4 fresh turkey legs	❏ ½ gallon hot water
	❏ 4 cups crushed ice
	❏ ½ cup Kosher salt
	❏ ½ cup brown sugar
	❏ 2 Tbsp peppercorns

Preparation:
1. In a large non-reactive bowl, combine water, salt and sugar until salt and sugar are dissolved. Add peppercorns and crushed ice and stir to combine.
2. Submerge the turkey legs in the brine and let sit in the fridge for 1 hour.
3. Remove from the brine and dry with a paper towel.
4. Let the turkey sit at room temperature while you preheat the smoker to 250°F.

Smoking:
1. Once the smoker is ready, place each turkey leg directly onto the grate.
2. Smoke the turkey legs until the internal temperature reaches 165°F.
3. Allow the legs to rest for 10-15 minutes before serving.

CHIPOTLE TURKEY LEGS

Serves: 4 | **Preparation Time:** Active - 10 minutes; Passive - 1 hour

A twist on the classic, these turkey legs get their tang from the chipotle mango lime barbecue sauce that is slathered on during the last hour of cooking.

Estimated Smoke Time: 4-5 hours
Smoke Temp: 250°F
Try these wood chips: Mesquite, Alder, Fruit wood

Ingredients:

Meat	Brine	Sauce
❏ 4 fresh turkey legs	❏ ½ gallon hot water ❏ 4 cups crushed ice ❏ ½ cup Kosher salt ❏ ½ cup brown sugar ❏ 2 Tbsp peppercorns	❏ 2 cups Chipotle Mango Lime Barbecue Sauce

Preparation:
1. In a large non-reactive bowl, combine water, salt and sugar until salt and sugar are dissolved. Add peppercorns and crushed ice and stir to combine.
2. Submerge the turkey legs in the brine and let sit in the fridge for 1 hour.
3. Remove from the brine and dry with a paper towel.
4. Let the turkey sit at room temperature while you preheat the smoker to 250°F.

Smoking:
1. Once the smoker is ready, place each turkey leg directly onto the grate.
2. Smoke the turkey legs until the internal temperature reaches 155°F.
3. Remove the legs from the smoker and brush on all sides with the Chipotle Mango Lime Barbecue Sauce.
4. Return the legs to the smoker and continue cooking until they reach an internal temperature of 165°F.
5. Remove the turkey legs from the smoker and allow the legs to rest for 10-15 minutes before serving with additional barbecue sauce on the side.

WHITE BEAN SOUP WITH SMOKED TURKEY

Serves: 8-10 | **Preparation Time:** 1 ½-2 hours

Traditionally, bean soup is made with ham hocks, pork shanks that have been cured and smoked. This soup relies on a smoked turkey leg for its rich broth. Bonus: the turkey meat falls off the bone and makes delightful meaty nuggets throughout the soup.

Ingredients:

Meat	Brine
❑ 1 smoked turkey leg	❑ 1 lb white beans (you can use any bean of your choosing)
	❑ 2 quarts water
	❑ 2 carrots
	❑ 2 bay leaves
	❑ 1 onion, finely diced
	❑ 1 rib of celery, finely diced
	❑ 1 tsp salt
	❑ ½ tsp black pepper

Preparation:

Meat

1. 1. In a large Dutch oven, heat olive oil over medium heat.
2. Add vegetables and season with salt and pepper.
3. Cook the vegetables until soft, about 7-8 minutes.
4. Add bay leaf, turkey leg, beans, and enough water to cover the beans by 2 inches (about 2 quarts).
5. Bring to a boil and reduce to a simmer. Cook for 1-1 ½ hours or until the beans are soft and the meat from the turkey leg is beginning to fall apart.
6. Remove the turkey leg, shred the meat, and return the meat to the pot, stirring to combine.
7. Serve with chunks of bread and your favorite hot sauce.

TIP: This soup can also be made in a slow cooker. Just place all ingredients in a 6 quart slow cooker (omit the oil) and cook on low for 4-6 hours.

GAME DAY CORNISH HENS

Serves: 4 | **Preparation Time:** Active - 10 minutes; Passive - 1-4 hours

Because of their size, cornish hens are perfect for tailgating. Adding beer and hot sauce to the brining liquid gives them the extra zip to score a touchdown at your next party.

Estimated Smoke Time: 1 ½ - 2 hours
Smoke Temp: 250°F
Try these wood chips: Mesquite, Alder, Fruit wood

Ingredients:

Meat	Brine
❑ 4 cornish hens	❑ ½ gallon hot water
	❑ 12 ounces cold beer
	❑ 4 cups crushed ice
	❑ ½ cup Kosher salt
	❑ ½ cup brown sugar
	❑ ¼ cup of your favorite hot sauce
	❑ 2 Tbsp peppercorns

Preparation:
1. In a large non-reactive bowl, combine water, salt and sugar until salt and sugar are dissolved. Add peppercorns, beer, hot sauce, and crushed ice and stir to combine.
2. Submerge the hens in the brine and let sit in the fridge for 1-4 hours.
3. Remove from the brine and dry with a paper towel.
4. Let the hens sit at room temperature while you preheat the smoker to 250°F.

Smoking:
1. Once the smoker is ready, place each hen directly onto the grate, breast side down.
2. Smoke the hens until the internal temperature at the thickest part of the thigh reaches 165°F.
3. Allow the hens to rest for 10-15 minutes before serving.

SEAFOOD

SMOKED LOBSTER

Smoked Lobster Roll
Smoked Lobster Bisque

SMOKED SHRIMP

Smoked Shrimp Po Boys
Spicy Butter Poached Smoked Shrimp
Garlicky Smoked Shrimp

SMOKED SALMON

Honey Chipotle Salmon With Pineapple
   Salsa
Smoked Salmon Frittata
Smoked Salmon Cheese Ball

SMOKED TROUT

Smoked Trout Chowder
Smoked Trout Breakfast Sandwiches
Smoked Trout Open-Faced Sandwiches
Smoked Trout and Tomato Salad

MARINATED SMOKED OYSTERS

Smoked Oysters Rockefeller
Linguini with Smoked Oysters
Smoked Oyster Bruschetta
Smoked Oyster Potato Salad

SMOKED LOBSTER

Serves: 4 | **Preparation Time:** 30 minutes

People don't generally associate lobster with anything other than boiling. But consider this, when you boil lobster, where does the flavor go? Into the boiling liquid. Smoking lobster, like roasting it, keeps the natural lobster flavor with the meat, making it richer and sweeter. This recipe uses a "compound butter" to flavor the lobster meat. It's just a fancy way of saying, "butter with yummy things in it". You can make the compound butter up to three days in advance.

Estimated Smoke Time: 45 minutes
Smoke Temp: 225°F
Try these wood chips: Alder, Pecan, Fruit Wood

Ingredients:

Meat	Brine
❏ 8 lobster tails ❏ 8 kebab skewers	❏ ½ cup (1 stick) butter, softened ❏ 1 clove garlic, finely minced ❏ 1 Tbs Money Rub ❏ 1 Tbs chopped chives

Preparation:
1. Preheat your smoker to 225°F
2. In a small bowl, combine butter, garlic, Money Rub, and chives until thoroughly combined. Set aside.
3. Using kitchen shears, cut along the back of the lobster tail shell.
4. Use your fingers to carefully separate the meat from the back of the shell.
5. Thread a kebab skewer through the underside of the tail from front to back. This keeps the lobster tail from curling during cooking.

Smoking:
1. Place the skewered lobster tails directly on the smoker grate.
2. Smoke until the lobster reaches 130°F.
3. Carefully spoon 1 Tbsp of the butter mixture onto the tail meat of each lobster.
4. Continue cooking until the lobsters reach 140°F.

SMOKED LOBSTER ROLLS

Serves: 4 | **Preparation Time:** 10 min

No trip to New England is complete without a lobster roll. The secret is in the bread. Finding split top lobster roll buns is nearly impossible outside of the northeast, but potato rolls make a fine substitute.

Ingredients:

Meat	Other
❏ 3 cups smoked lobster meat, chopped	❏ 4 lobster roll buns, buttered and toasted
	❏ ¼ cup mayonnaise
	❏ 2 Tbsp finely diced celery
	❏ 2 Tbsp finely diced scallion
	❏ ½ tsp hot sauce (we like Tabasco for this)

Preparation:

1. In a medium bowl, gently combine lobster, celery, scallion, mayonnaise, and hot sauce.
2. Generously spoon the mixture onto toasted lobster roll buns.
3. Eat with napkins and cold beer for the full New England experience.

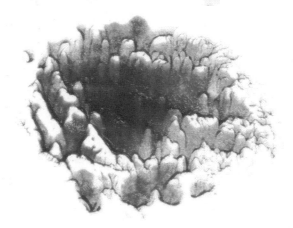

SMOKED LOBSTER BISQUE

Serves: 4 | **Preparation Time:** 2 hours

Do not throw away your lobster shells! This delicious soup is ideal for getting the most out of those tasty crustaceans.

Ingredients:

Stock	Other
❑ 8 smoked lobster tail shells	❑ 1 cup finely diced onion
❑ 8 cups water	❑ 1 cup heavy cream
	❑ ½ cup finely diced carrot
	❑ ½ cup finely diced celery
	❑ ¼ cup tomato paste
	❑ ½ cup sherry
	❑ 2 Tbsp leftover compound butter (or extra-virgin olive oil)
	❑ 2 sprigs of fresh thyme
	❑ Any leftover lobster meat

Preparation:

1. In a large stockpot, combine lobster tail shells and water. Bring it to a boil and reduce it to a simmer for 1 hour.
2. Strain out lobster shells and any sediment in the broth, reserving the lobster stock.
3. In the same large stockpot, melt compound butter over medium heat until foamy.
4. Add vegetables and thyme and cook until softened, about 7-8 minutes.
5. Add tomato paste and cook 2-3 minutes until it turns dark red.
6. Add sherry and cook for 2-3 minutes or until it is reduced by half.
7. Add half of the lobster stock and stir together. Cook until vegetables are completely soft, around 20 minutes.
8. Pour soup into a blender and blend until smooth. Return the soup to the pot.
9. Add remaining lobster stock, stir in heavy cream and simmer on low 20 minutes more.
10. Dish soup into bowls with chopped smoked lobster tail on top.

SMOKED SHRIMP

Serves: 4 | **Preparation Time:** Active - 2 minutes; Inactive - 20 minutes

When it comes to seafood, shrimp have a built-in thermometer. When they are pink and slightly curled, they are ready to eat. We love "easy peel" shrimp because they are already deveined but still have the shell on. This helps the shrimp retain their moisture without having to go through the trouble of deveining them.

Estimated Smoke Time: 12-15 minutes
Smoke Temp: 225°F
Try these wood chips: Alder

Ingredients:

Meat	Rub
❏ 2 lbs "easy peel" shrimp	❏ 2 Tbsp Money Rub

Preparation:
1. In a large, zip top bag, combine rub and shrimp. Seal the bag and shake to completely coat the shrimp.
2. Refrigerate shrimp for 20 minutes.
3. Preheat smoker to 225°F

Smoking:
1. Place shrimp in a single layer on a baking sheet.
2. Place the baking sheet in the smoker and cook until shrimp are pink and begin to curl, about 12-15 minutes.

SMOKED SHRIMP PO BOYS

Serves: 4 | **Preparation Time:** 10 min

"Po Boy" sandwiches are all over the deep south. Made with cornbread coated shrimp, oysters, or clams, these sandwiches are delicious in their own right. Our Po Boy uses smoked shrimp for a lighter texture and a fewer calories.

Ingredients:

Meat	Other
❏ 1 lb Garlicky Smoked Shrimp, peeled	❏ 4 hoagie rolls
	❏ 8 slices tomato
	❏ 2 cups shredded lettuce
	❏ ¼ cup mayonnaise mixed with
	❏ 1 tsp hot sauce

Preparation:

1. Split hoagie rolls and spread with mayonnaise and hot sauce mixture.
2. Top rolls with Garlicky Smoked Shrimp, lettuce, and tomato

SPICY BUTTER POACHED SMOKED SHRIMP

Serves: 4 | **Preparation Time:** 10 min

Butter poaching seafood is not only decadent, it is a surefire way to make sure the shrimp stays tender.

Estimated Smoke Time: 30 minutes
Smoke Temp: 275°F
Try these wood chips: Alder, Fruit Wood

Ingredients:

Meat	Other
❏ 2 lbs "easy peel" shrimp	❏ 1 lb (4 sticks) of butter
	❏ 1 Tbsp lemon zest
	❏ 1 Tbsp lemon juice
	❏ 2 tsp hot sauce (we like sriracha)
	❏ 2 tsp Chile Rub
	❏ 1 tsp Worcestershire sauce
	❏ 1 garlic clove, lightly smashed

Preparation:

1. In a saucepan, melt butter with remaining ingredients. Set aside.
2. Preheat smoker to 275°F.
3. In an aluminum pan, arrange the shrimp then pour butter mixture over them.

Smoking:

1. Place the aluminum pan in the smoker and cook for 30 minutes or until the shrimp become pink.
2. Serve shrimp and butter with large chunks of bread.

GARLICKY SMOKED SHRIMP

Serves: 4 | **Preparation Time:** Active - 5 minutes; Passive - 30 minutes

Think of this dish like shrimp scampi, minus the butter. These shrimp are so flavorful, you won't even miss it.

Estimated Smoke Time: 12-15 minutes
Smoke Temp: 225°F
Try these wood chips: Alder, Fruit wood

Ingredients:

Meat	Rub
❏ 2 lbs "easy peel" shrimp	❏ ¼ cup olive oil
	❏ 2 Tbsp lemon zest
	❏ 4 cloves garlic, minced
	❏ 1 small shallot, minced
	❏ ½ tsp salt
	❏ ¼ tsp black pepper
	❏ ¼ tsp hot sauce

Preparation:

1. In a large, zip top bag, combine rub ingredients and shrimp and refrigerate for 30 minutes.
2. Preheat the smoker to 225°F.

Smoking:

1. Arrange the shrimp directly on the smoker grates and cook for 12-15 minutes or until the shrimp turn pink.

Note: You can arrange the shrimp on skewers for easy removal or smoke the shrimp in a shallow aluminum pan.

SMOKED SALMON

Serves: 8 | **Preparation Time:** Active - 15 minutes; Passive - 3 hours

There are two types of smoked salmon commonly consumed in the United States - cold smoked salmon or gravlax, and hot smoked salmon. For now, we will deal exclusively in hot smoked salmon. Buy the freshest salmon you can find. It should be glossy, firm, and smell like the ocean.

Estimated Smoke Time: 45 minutes
Smoke Temp: 225°F
Try these wood chips: Fruit Woods, Mesquite

Ingredients:

Meat	Brine
❑ 2 lbs fresh salmon	❑ ½ gallon warm water
	❑ ½ cup Kosher Salt
	❑ ¼ cup granulated white sugar
	❑ 4 whole garlic cloves, lightly smashed
	❑ 2 Tbsp finely ground black pepper

Preparation:
1. In a large, non-reactive bowl, combine salt, sugar, black pepper, and water and stir until salt and sugar dissolve. Add garlic.
2. Place salmon and brine in a large ziptop bag, set inside another pan in case the bag leaks.
3. Seal bag and allow the fish to sit, fully submerged, in the brine for 3 hours.
4. Preheat the smoker to 225°F.

Smoking:
1. Pat the salmon filets dry and place the fish, skin side down, on parchment paper before placing on the smoker racks.
2. Smoke the salmon until it reaches an internal temperature of 140°F.
3. Remove from smoker and allow the salmon to sit for 10 minutes before serving.

HONEY CHIPOTLE SALMON WITH PINEAPPLE SALSA

Serves: 4 | **Preparation Time:** Active - 20 minutes; Passive - 1 hour

Salmon is one of the only fish that can stand up to big, bold flavors. And this dish is big and bold. Sweet, smoky, spicy, big, and bold to be exact.

Estimated Smoke Time: 45 minutes
Smoke Temp: 225°F
Try these wood chips: Mesquite

Ingredients:

Meat	Rub & Sauce	Pineapple Salsa
❑ 2 lbs salmon, cut into 4 pieces	❑ 2 Tbsp Classic American ❑ Brown Sugar Rub ❑ ¼ cup Honey Chipotle ❑ Barbecue Sauce	❑ 1 cup fresh or canned pineapple, minced ❑ 1 cup red bell pepper, minced ❑ ½ cup red onion, minced ❑ ½ cup fresh lime juice ❑ 1 Tbsp cilantro, finely chopped ❑ 1 Tbsp extra-virgin olive oil

Preparation:

1. In a small bowl, combine all salsa ingredients and set aside.
2. Liberally apply Classic American Brown Sugar Rub to the flesh side of the salmon. Cover and refrigerate for 1 hour.
3. Remove the salmon from the fridge and preheat the smoker to 225°F

Smoking:

1. Place salmon, skin side down, on a piece of parchment that has been placed over the grates of the smoker.
2. Smoke for 30 minutes or until the salmon has reached an internal temperature of 130°F.
3. Remove the salmon from the smoker and brush liberally with Honey Chipotle Barbecue Sauce.
4. Return the salmon to the smoker and continue cooking until it reaches an internal temperature of 140°F.
5. Allow the salmon to sit for 10 minutes before topping with pineapple salsa and serving.

SMOKED SALMON FRITTATA

Serves: 6 | **Preparation Time:** 1 hour

Smoked salmon and eggs go very well together. This traditional smoked salmon frittata can also be made into soft scrambled eggs by skipping the baking step in this recipe.

Ingredients:

Meat	Other
❏ ½ pound smoked salmon, chopped	❏ 12 large eggs
	❏ 1 cup whole milk
	❏ 1 medium onion, finely diced
	❏ 3 Tbsp chopped, fresh dill
	❏ 1 Tbsp butter
	❏ 1 tsp Kosher salt
	❏ ½ tsp black pepper

Preparation:

1. In a 10-inch oven-proof skillet, melt butter and saute onion until translucent, about 7-8 minutes.
2. Whisk together eggs, milk, dill, salt and pepper until thoroughly combined. Gently stir in the smoked salmon.
3. Pour the egg mixture into the skillet and place in a preheated 350°F oven for 50 minutes.
4. Remove from the oven and serve warm, straight out of the pan.

SMOKED SALMON CHEESE BALL

Serves: 10 | **Preparation Time:** 10 minutes plus chilling time

Cheese balls were all the rage in the 80s. Simple to make and endlessly customizable, cheese balls are ideal snacks for a crowd. You can make this cheese ball up to a day in advance to allow all of the flavors to get to know each other.

Ingredients:

Meat	Other
❏ ½ pound smoked salmon, finely chopped	❏ 1 8-oz package cream cheese, softened ❏ ¼ cup chopped parsley ❏ 3 Tbsp scallions, finely chopped ❏ 1 Tbsp fresh dill, chopped (or 1 tsp dried) ❏ 1 tsp lemon juice ❏ ½ tsp Worcestershire sauce ❏ ½ tsp hot sauce ❏ Crackers, bagel chips, or vegetables for serving

Preparation:

1. In a medium sized bowl, mix together cream cheese, salmon, scallions, dill, lemon juice, Worcestershire sauce, and hot sauce until thoroughly combined.
2. Scrape the cream cheese mixture onto a large piece of plastic wrap.
3. Using the edges of the plastic wrap, form the cheese mixture into a ball. Wrap tightly and refrigerate for 1 hour.
4. Before serving, remove cheese ball from the fridge and roll in chopped parsley.

SMOKED TROUT

Makes: 2 lbs smoked trout | **Preparation Time:** 3 hours

Trout is found in cool streams and lakes throughout the United States. However, trout is also known for having a strong, fishy flavor and smell. Smoking the trout tones down the fishy flavor, replacing it with smoky goodness. And while smoked trout is delicious on its own, it makes a lovely flavoring agent for soups and salads.

Estimated Smoke Time: 2 ½-3 hours
Smoke Temp: 160°F
Try these wood chips: Hickory, mesquite

Ingredients:

Meat	Brine
❏ 2 lbs trout filets	❏ 1 quart water
	❏ ½ cup Kosher salt
	❏ ½ cup brown sugar

Preparation:
1. Stir together the water, salt, and sugar in a 4 quart glass dish until salt is dissolved.
2. Submerge trout filets in the brine, cover, and refrigerate for 3 hours.
3. Preheat the smoker to 160°F.
4. Remove the trout from the brine, pat dry.

Smoking:
1. Place the trout filets directly on the smoker grate.
2. Smoke the trout files until they reach an internal temperature of 145°F.

SMOKED TROUT CHOWDER

Serves: 4 | **Preparation Time:** 30 minutes

Smoked trout gives this chowder the briney flavor of New England clam chowder, without the clams. Brothy and delicious, this chowder is the perfect way to beat the chill in the air.

Ingredients:

Meat	Other
❏ 2 fillets smoked trout, skin removed, fish flaked	❏ 1 pound baking potatoes (about 2), peeled and cut into 1/2-inch cubes
	❏ 1 quart canned low-sodium chicken broth or homemade stock
	❏ 2 cups water
	❏ 1 cup half-and-half
	❏ 1 cup frozen corn
	❏ 6 scallions, chopped
	❏ 2 ribs celery, chopped
	❏ 2 cloves garlic, minced
	❏ ¼ cup dry white wine
	❏ 1 Tbsp butter
	❏ 1 tsp dried thyme
	❏ 1 ¼ tsp salt
	❏ 1 bay leaf

Preparation:

1. In a large stock pot, melt butter until foamy.
2. Cook celery, the white sections of the scallions, and garlic until soft and translucent, about 5 minutes.
3. Add wine, water, and stock along with potatoes, thyme, bay, and salt.
4. Bring to a boil then reduce to a simmer and cook the potatoes until they are soft, about 20 minutes.
5. Add half and half, frozen corn, trout, and green parts of the scallions and continue cooking an additional 5 minutes until the soup is hot.
6. Serve immediately with chunks of bread.

SMOKED TROUT BREAKFAST SANDWICHES

Serves: 2 | **Preparation Time:** 10 min

Smoked trout and eggs go extremely well together. Layer the mixture on an everything bagel and you will think you have died and gone to breakfast heaven.

Ingredients:

Meat	Other
❏ 1 smoked trout fillet, lightly flaked	❏ 4 large eggs
	❏ 2 Tbsp heavy cream
	❏ 2 Tbsp shredded Swiss cheese
	❏ 1 Tbsp butter
	❏ 1 scallion, finely chopped
	❏ ¼ tsp prepared horseradish (optional)
	❏ 1 Everything bagel, lightly toasted
	❏ Salt and pepper to taste

Preparation:

1. In a medium-sized non-stick skillet, heat butter until foamy over medium heat.
2. Add scallion and saute 1 minute.
3. In a small bowl, whisk together eggs, cream, and horseradish. Add to the skillet.
4. Reduce the heat to medium-low and stir eggs constantly until they begin to set.
5. Add smoked trout, Swiss cheese, salt and pepper, and stir to combine.
6. Remove the eggs from the heat and divide between the two halves of the everything bagel.
7. Serve open-faced.

SMOKED TROUT OPEN-FACED SANDWICHES

Serves: 4 | **Preparation Time:** 5 min

These simple open-faced sandwiches are ideal for cutting into smaller pieces and serving during a cocktail party. Or pair them with a green salad for a quick, easy, flavorful lunch.

Ingredients:

Meat	Other
❑ 4 ounces smoked trout	❑ 4 sliced pumpernickel bread, toasted
	❑ ½ cup sour cream
	❑ ¼ cup dill, chopped
	❑ 1 tsp Dijon mustard
	❑ Baby arugula
	❑ Sliced radishes

Preparation:

1. In a small bowl, mix together trout, dill, sour cream, and Dijon mustard. Season with salt and pepper to taste.
2. Spread 2 Tbsp of the mixture on each slice of pumpernickel. Top with radish slices, baby arugula, and a drizzle of extra-virgin olive oil.

SMOKED TROUT AND TOMATO SALAD

Serves: 2 | **Preparation Time:** 10 min

If you are looking for a light summer salad, look no further than this satisfying lunch. Or double the recipe and serve it as a side dish at your next summer potluck.

Ingredients:

Meat	Other
❏ 4 ounces smoked trout, flaked	❏ 2 cups sweet corn (fresh or frozen)
	❏ 2 large tomatoes, diced
	❏ 1 medium onion, chopped
	❏ 2 Tbsp extra-virgin olive oil
	❏ 2 Tbsp fresh basil, chopped
	❏ 1 Tbsp balsamic vinegar
	❏ Salt and pepper to taste

Preparation:
1. In a large saute pan, heat extra-virgin olive oil over medium heat.
2. Add onion and cook until translucent, about 5-6 minutes.
3. Pour the corn kernels into the pan and cook 2-3 minutes more. Set aside to cool.
4. In a bowl, combine tomatoes, basil, vinegar, salt and pepper, and the warm corn and onion mixture.
5. Gently fold in the flaked trout and serve.

MARINATED SMOKED OYSTERS

Serves: 4 | Preparation Time: 1 hour

Canned smoked oysters have been considered a delicacy in the United States for hundreds of years. Because they were expensive, they were generally reserved for special occasions. These smoked oysters are far better than their canned counterparts and since you control your brine and your marinade, you don't have to worry about pesky preservatives. It is certainly possible to smoke oysters on the half shell, but oysters marinated in olive oil will keep in the fridge for up to a week. Just remember to keep them as cold as possible at all times.

Estimated Smoke Time: 30-45 minutes
Smoke Temp: 225°F
Try these wood chips: Alder, mesquite

Ingredients:

Meat	Brine	Marinade
❏ 48 medium-sized oysters (about 5-7" in the shell), shucked	❏ ½ gallon water ❏ ½ cup brown sugar ❏ ¼ cup Kosher salt ❏ 1 bay leaf ❏ 1 tsp garlic powder ❏ 1 tsp black pepper	❏ 4 cloves garlic, lightly mashed ❏ 2 cups extra-virgin olive oil ❏ 1 tsp crushed red pepper flakes

Preparation:
1. In a small saucepan, heat olive oil, garlic, and red pepper flakes over low heat for 20 minutes. Set aside to cool.
2. In a large, nonreactive bowl, stir brine ingredients together until salt and sugar dissolves.
3. Add 4 cups of ice and oysters to the brine and refrigerate for 30-40 minutes.
4. Preheat smoker to 225°F.
5. Remove oysters from the fridge and rinse under cold water to remove any remaining seasoning or sediment.
6. Place the oysters on sheet trays so they are not touching and slide the trays into the smoker.

Smoking:
1. Smoke the oysters at 225°F until the edges begin to curl, around 30-45 minutes.
2. Remove the oysters from the smoker and immediately pour into a large plastic container filled with the infused olive oil mixture. Stir to combine.

Note: Allow the oysters to marinate in the olive oil, in the fridge, for 1-2 hours before serving. They will only get better as they sit. Serve with crackers, or use in any of the smoked oyster recipes in this book.

SMOKED OYSTERS ROCKEFELLER

Serves: 8 as an appetizer | **Preparation Time:** 1 hour

For this recipe, you will shuck and then smoke the oysters on the halfshell. This will give you a vessel to hold the delicious filling that will finish off this classic dish.

Estimated Smoke Time: 30-45 minutes
Smoke Temp: 225°F
Try these wood chips: Alder

Ingredients:

Meat	Other
❏ 2 dozen oysters, shucked, then placed on the half shell	❏ 2 cups chopped fresh spinach
	❏ 1/3cup bread crumbs, Panko preferred
	❏ ¼ cup (½ stick) butter
	❏ ¼ cup dry white wine
	❏ ¼ cup grated Parmesan
	❏ 2 shallots, chopped
	❏ 2 garlic cloves, minced
	❏ Salt and pepper, to taste
	❏ Dash hot sauce

Preparation:

1. Place oysters on the half shell on a sheet pan and refrigerate to keep cold.
2. Preheat the smoker to 225°F.
   While the oysters are smoking:
3. In a skillet, heat butter and garlic over low heat until the garlic turns translucent, about 3-4 minutes.
4. Pour half of the garlic butter mixture over bread crumbs in a small bowl. Stir until the breadcrumbs are evenly coated with the garlic butter.
5. Add parmesan cheese to the breadcrumb mixture and stir to combine.
6. Return the skillet with the remaining garlic butter to the stove and add shallots.
7. Cook the shallots over medium heat until translucent.
8. Pile chopped spinach into the pan and allow it to wilt.
9. When the spinach has completely wilted, add wine and cook 2-3 minutes or until the wine has reduced by half. Turn off the heat and allow the spinach to cool slightly.

Smoking:

1. Place the sheet tray of oysters into the smoker.
2. Smoke the oysters until the edges begin to curl, about 30-45 minutes.

Assembly:

1. Spoon 1 Tbsp of the spinach mixture onto each oyster and top with parmesan and breadcrumb mixture.
2. Place oysters under the broiler for 1 minute or until the breadcrumbs and cheese brown.
3. Serve hot.

LINGUINE WITH SMOKED OYSTERS

Serves: 8 | **Preparation Time:** 45 minutes

If you look at many pasta sauce recipes, you are two-thirds of the way there with marinated smoked oysters. Olive oil? Check. Garlic? Check. Crushed red pepper? Check. Add some delicious smoked oysters and a few other ingredients and you have a fast, delicious, satisfying meal.

Ingredients:

Meat	Other
❑ 4 ounces Marinated Smoked Oysters, chopped	❑ 1 lb dried linguine
	❑ ¼ cup grated parmesan cheese
	❑ 3 Tbsp smoked oyster marinade
	❑ 2 Tbsp chopped parsley
	❑ 1 Tbsp capers
	❑ 2 cloves garlic, minced
	❑ Crushed red pepper flake to taste

Preparation:

1. Prepare linguine according to the package directions, reserving ¼ cup of the salty pasta water.
2. In a large skillet over medium heat, heat oyster marinade with garlic, capers and crushed red pepper flake until garlic is light brown. Add oysters for 1 minute.
3. Add hot pasta, the pasta water, parmesan cheese and chopped parsley and stir to combine off of the heat.
4. Serve with additional parmesan cheese.

SMOKED OYSTER BRUSCHETTA

Serves: 8 | **Preparation Time:** 20 min

Thick slices of lightly toasted bread are merely the vehicle to bring the caramelized onion cream cheese and smoked oyster to your mouth. A vehicle you will gladly drive again and again.

Ingredients:

Meat	Other
❏ 16 smoked oysters	❏ 1 baguette, sliced 1-inch thick into 16 slices
	❏ 8 ounces of cream cheese, softened
	❏ 1 medium onion, finely diced
	❏ ¼ cup oyster marinade
	❏ 2 Tbsp butter
	❏ ¼ tsp black pepper

Preparation:

1. In a large skillet over medium-low heat, melt butter and add onion.
2. Cook together until onion turns translucent then begins to caramelize, about 10 minutes. Set aside to cool.
3. Brush each baguette slice with oyster marinade and lightly toast under a broiler for 1 minute. (This can be done on a grill.)
4. Combine cream cheese, black pepper, and caramelized onion.
5. Spread each bread slice with the cream cheese mixture and to with a smoked oyster. Serve immediately.

SMOKED OYSTER POTATO SALAD

Serves: 4 | **Preparation Time:** 30 min

Everyone has a favorite potato salad. This just may become yours. Since this salad does not have any mayonnaise, it is ideal for summer potlucks.

Ingredients:

Meat	Other
❏ 4 ounces smoked oysters, chopped	❏ ¾ pound small red or fingerling potatoes
	❏ 2 cups arugula
	❏ 1 celery rib, thinly sliced
	❏ ¼ red onion, thinly sliced
	❏ 2 Tbsp smoked oyster marinade
	❏ 2 Tbsp fresh lemon juice

Preparation:

1. In a large saucepan, cover the potatoes by 1 inch with cold, salted water.
2. Bring the water to a boil, reduce it to a simmer, and allow the potatoes to cook until fork tender, about 12-15 minutes.
3. Drain the potatoes well and slice into ⬚ inch wide rounds.
4. Toss potatoes with the remaining ingredients and serve.

Tip: If you are making this salad and transporting it to a party, reserve the arugula for tossing in just before serving.

COLD SMOKING RECIPES

COLD SMOKED BACON

BEEF JERKY

COLD SMOKED CHEESE

Smo-Fried Mozzarella Cheese Sticks
Smoked Brie & Apricot Preserves

COLD SMOKED NUTS

Smoked Almonds
Sweet and Spicy Smoked Pecans
Smoked Cocktail Peanuts
Candied Walnuts
Rosemary Smoked Cashews

COLD SMOKED SALMON

SMOKED VEGETABLES

Cold Smoked Tomato Salsa
Smoked Cabbage Steaks With Dijon
　　Vinaigrette

DESSERTS

Calypso Banana Splits
Smoked Figs With Marscapone
Smoked Pineapple With Honey
Nutella S'Mores Dip

COLD SMOKED BACON

Makes: 3 lbs bacon | **Preparation Time:** 1 week

Cold smoking meats at home is not recommended by the USDA. Holding meat in the "danger zone" (between 40°F and 130°F) invites bacteria growth. However, cold smoking bacon that is cured, then later thoroughly cooked, is not only considered safe, but delicious. This particular recipe calls for a specialized ingredient called "Prague Powder #1", a curing salt that contains salt and sodium nitrate and is ideal for home curing meats. It is available at sporting good stores, butcher shops, and online retailers.

Estimated Smoke Time: 6-8 hours
Smoke Temp: 75°F
Try these wood chips: Maple, Hickory

Ingredients:

Meat	Cure
❑ 3 lbs pork belly	❑ ¾ cup distilled water
	❑ 6 Tbsp dark brown sugar
	❑ 2 Tbsp kosher salt
	❑ 3 tsp black pepper
	❑ 1 ½ tsp Prague Powder #1

Preparation:
1. Rinse the pork belly and pat-dry with a paper towel.
2. In a large zip top bag, combine cure ingredients.
3. Submerge pork belly into the bag and close, placing the bag in a container in the refrigerator for 7 days, making sure to flip the bag over every day and massage the pork belly to redistribute the spices.
4. Remove the pork belly from the fridge and thoroughly wash it under cold water to stop the curing process.
5. Sprinkle the slab generously with freshly ground pepper, if you want a pepper bacon.
6. Let it sit at room temperature while preheating the smoker to 75°F.

Smoking:
1. Place the pork belly directly on the smoker grate, fat side up.
2. Smoke the pork belly for 6-8 hours. The smoke will not penetrate the meat as quickly at a lower temperature, and the meat itself will not go above 75°F.
3. Remove the bacon from the smoker and wrap tightly in plastic wrap. Wrap in foil and chill in the refrigerator for 24 hours before slicing and using.

BEEF JERKY

Makes: 2 lbs jerky | **Preparation Time:** Active - 10 minutes; Passive - 24 hours

Beef Jerky is traditionally made in a food dehydrator. Our beef jerky has the added bonus of a luscious smoky flavor that you can't get in a normal dehydrator. Start the beef in a cold smoker and allow it to come to temperature with the beef inside. Your end temperature of 155°F may not seem like "cold smoking" but it is warm enough to dry the meat out without cooking it. If you like your jerky spicy, add cayenne to your marinade. If you enjoy pepper jerky, add 1 tsp black pepper to the marinade.

Estimated Smoke Time: 12 hours
Smoke Temp: Varies
Try these wood chips: Mesquite, Hickory

Ingredients:

Meat	Marinade
❏ 2 ½ lbs beef eye of round, sliced 3/16" thick across the grain. (Your butcher will be happy to do this for you.)	❏ 1 bottle pre-made teriyaki sauce ❏ 3 Tbsp fresh ginger ❏ 2 Tbsp Salt and Pepper Beef Rub

Preparation:
1. In a large, zip top bag, combine marinade and meat and refrigerate for 24 hours.
2. Shake off any excess marinade and arrange the meat directly on the smoker grates.

Smoking:
1. Turn on the smoker and set it to 100°F for 1 hour.
2. Increase the temperature to 110°F for 1 hour.
3. Increase the temperature to 120°F for 1 hour.
4. Increase the temperature to 130°F for 1 hour.
5. Increase the temperature to 140°F for 1 hour.
6. Increase the temperature to 155°F for 7 hours.
7. Remove the jerky from the smoker and allow it to cool before storing in a zip top bag.

COLD SMOKED CHEESE

Preparation Time: 5 min

There are a few things all smoked cheese have in common. The most important of which is the fact that all need to sit in the refrigerator for a minimum of 48 hours before serving to allow the smoke flavor to mellow. Unlike meat, cheese eaten right off of the smoker tends to be bitter and resting gives the smoke flavor a chance to develop throughout the cheese. All cheeses can be smoked using this method.

Estimated Smoke Time: 2 hours
Smoke Temp: 80°F
Try these wood chips: Apple wood

Ingredients:

❏ 1 lb block or wheel of cheese

Preparation:

1. Remove the cheese from the refrigerator 15-20 minutes before smoking.
2. Preheat the smoker to 80°F.
3. Fill an aluminum pan with ice and cover with a wire rack.
4. Place the cheese on top of the wire rack.

Smoking:

1. Smoke the cheese in the smoker for 2 hours.
2. Remove from the smoker and allow it to rest for 1 hour on the counter.
3. Wipe excess oils from the surface of the cheese, wrap in plastic wrap and refrigerate for 3-4 days before using.

Tip: To smoke cheese sticks, space them with ½ inch space between and reduce the smoking time to 15 minutes.

SMO-FRIED MOZZARELLA CHEESE STICKS

Serves: 2 | Preparation Time: 30 min

It is nearly impossible to pass up deep fried cheese. These delightful little nuggets of goodness are made easier by using smoked mozzarella cheese sticks.

Ingredients:

Cheese	Breading	Sauce
❑ 4 smoked mozzarella cheese sticks	❑ 2 cups Italian seasoned Panko ❑ breadcrumbs ❑ 2 eggs, lightly beaten ❑ ¼ cup flour ❑ 1 Tbsp water ❑ ¼ tsp salt ❑ ¼ tsp pepper ❑ Vegetable Oil for frying	❑ 1 cup of your favorite marinara or barbecue sauce, warmed

Preparation:
1. Cut each cheese stick into four equal pieces.
2. Arrange three shallow dishes side by side.
3. Fill the first dish with flour, salt and pepper and stir to combine.
4. Mix together the eggs and water in the second dish.
5. Pour the seasoned Panko in the third.
6. Dip each piece of cheese into the flour, then eggs, then Panko and place on a wire rack positioned over a baking sheet.
7. Chill the breaded cheese for 10 minutes while the oil heats.
8. In a large saucepan, heat 1 ½ inches of vegetable oil to 350°F.
9. Drop 4-6 pieces of cheese at a time into the oil and cook until golden brown.
10. Move to paper towels and season with additional salt while they are hot.
11. Serve with dipping sauce.

SMOKED BRIE & APRICOT PRESERVES

Serves: 6 | **Preparation Time:** 10 min

Smoking a small brie wheel adds a level of complexity to the creamy, tangy cheese. Pairing it with apricot preserves is the perfect choice for an unbelievable appetizer.

Ingredients:
- ❏ 1 8-ounce wheel of Smoked Brie
- ❏ ½ cup apricot preserves
- ❏ 2 Tbsp sliced almonds
- ❏ ¼ tsp cayenne pepper
- ❏ Crackers for serving

Preparation:
1. Preheat oven to 400°F.
2. Slice the top of rind off of the cheese and place it in an oven-safe baking dish.
3. Stir together apricot preserves and cayenne pepper and spread on top of the cheese.
4. Top with sliced almonds and bake 10-12 minutes or until the cheese is melted.
5. Serve immediately with crackers.

COLD SMOKED NUTS

Serves: 16 | **Preparation Time:** 10 min

Cold smoking nuts couldn't be easier. You could throw roasted, salted nuts on the smoker for 2-3 hours and wind up with a yummy, lightly smoked nut. You could even smoke seasoned nuts at a higher temperature (225°F) and skip the roasting step altogether. For our purposes, we will smoke nuts then finish them in the oven with tasty surprises.

Estimated Smoke Time: 30 minutes
Smoke Temp: 90°F
Try these wood chips: Mesquite

Ingredients:

Nuts	Brine
❏ 1 lb raw nuts	❏ 4 cups room temperature water
	❏ ¼ cup Kosher salt

Preparation:
1. In a medium-sized non-reactive bowl, mix water and salt until salt dissolves.
2. Add nuts and allow them to soak for 10 minutes.
3. Arrange the nuts on a sheet tray.
4. Preheat the smoker to 90°F

Smoking:
1. Smoke the nuts for 30 minutes.

Finishing:
1. To finish the nuts, place in a 300°F oven for 15-20 minutes, stirring often.

SMOKED ALMONDS

Serves: 16 | **Preparation Time:** 10 min

Almonds are one of the most versatile nuts out there. Loaded with healthy fats, smoked almonds are not only tasty, they are a nutrient dense alternative to chips or pretzels.

Estimated Smoke Time: 30 minutes
Smoke Temp: 90°F
Try these wood chips: Apple or cherry

Ingredients:

Nuts	Brine	Finishing Spices
❑ 1 lb raw almonds	❑ 4 cups water, room temperature ❑ ¼ cup Kosher salt	❑ 2 Tbsp extra-virgin olive oil ❑ 1 Tbsp kosher salt finely ground (coarse salt doesn't stick to the almonds very well) ❑ 2 tsp chili powder ❑ 1 tsp fresh ground black pepper ❑ ½ tsp garlic powder ❑ ¼ tsp cayenne pepper

Preparation:
1. In a medium-sized non-reactive bowl, mix water and salt until salt dissolves.
2. Add nuts and allow them to soak for 10 minutes.
3. Arrange the nuts on a sheet tray.
4. Preheat the smoker to 90°F

Smoking:
1. Smoke the nuts for 30 minutes.

Finishing:
1. In a large bowl, mix together finishing spices and olive oil.
2. Toss in smoked nuts and stir to thoroughly combine.
3. Bake in a sheet tray at 375°F for 15 minutes, stirring often.
4. Allow the nuts to thoroughly cool before serving.

SWEET AND SPICY SMOKED PECANS

Serves: 16 | Preparation Time: 10 min

These Sweet and Spicy Smoked Pecans will satisfy even the toughest snack craving.

Estimated Smoke Time: 30 minutes
Smoke Temp: 90°F
Try these wood chips: Apple or cherry

Ingredients:

Nuts	Brine	Finishing
❑ 1 lb raw pecans	❑ 4 cups water, room temperature ❑ ¼ cup Kosher salt	❑ ¼ cup real maple syrup ❑ 2 Tbsp butter, melted ❑ ½ tsp ginger powder ❑ ¼ tsp cayenne pepper

Preparation:
1. In a medium-sized non-reactive bowl, mix water and salt until salt dissolves.
2. Add nuts and allow them to soak for 10 minutes.
3. Arrange the nuts on a sheet tray.
4. Preheat the smoker to 90°F

Smoking:
1. Smoke the nuts for 30 minutes.

Finishing:
1. In a large bowl, combine finishing ingredients.
2. Toss smoked nuts with the finishing ingredients and place on a lightly greased sheet tray.
3. Bake at 375°F for 15-20 minutes, stirring frequently.
4. Allow the nuts to cool completely before serving.

SMOKED COCKTAIL PEANUTS

Serves: 16 | **Preparation Time:** 10 min

These aren't your ordinary bar snack. These peanuts are dusted with a spicy seasoning that will leave you coming back for more.

Estimated Smoke Time: 30 minutes
Smoke Temp: 90°F
Try these wood chips: Apple or cherry

Ingredients:

Nuts	Brine	Finishing
❏ 1 lb raw peanuts	❏ 4 cups water, room temperature ❏ ¼ cup Kosher salt	❏ 2 Tbsp vegetable oil ❏ 1 tsp granulated garlic ❏ 1 tsp Cajun Rub ❏ ½ tsp table salt

Preparation:
1. In a medium-sized non-reactive bowl, mix water and salt until salt dissolves.
2. Add nuts and allow them to soak for 10 minutes.
3. Arrange the nuts on a sheet tray.
4. Preheat the smoker to 90°F

Smoking:
1. Smoke the nuts for 30 minutes.

Finishing:
1. In a large bowl, combine oil, garlic, Cajun Rub, and salt.
2. Toss in smoked peanuts and stir to combine.
3. Spread the nuts on a sheet tray and bake at 375°F for 15 minutes, stirring frequently.
4. Allow the nuts to cool completely before serving.

CANDIED WALNUTS

Serves: 16 | Preparation Time: 10 min

These nuts not only make a great snack, they are also delicious on salads and desserts. You should probably make a double batch.

Estimated Smoke Time: 30 minutes
Smoke Temp: 90°F
Try these wood chips: Apple or cherry

Cold Smoked Nuts

Ingredients:

Nuts	Brine	Finishing
❑ 1 lb raw walnuts	❑ 4 cups water, room temperature ❑ ¼ cup Kosher salt	❑ ½ cup brown sugar ❑ 3 Tbsp maple syrup ❑ 2 Tbsp melted butter ❑ 2 tsp table salt ❑ 1 tsp cinnamon powder

Preparation:
1. In a medium-sized non-reactive bowl, mix water and salt until salt dissolves.
2. Add nuts and allow them to soak for 10 minutes.
3. Arrange the nuts on a sheet tray.
4. Preheat the smoker to 90°F

Smoking:
1. Smoke the nuts for 30 minutes.

Finishing:
1. In a large bowl, combine finishing ingredients and toss in smoked walnuts.
2. Stir thoroughly to combine and pour onto a greased sheet tray.
3. Bake at 250°F for 20-30 minutes, stirring every 5 minutes.
4. Allow the nuts to cool thoroughly before serving.

ROSEMARY SMOKED CASHEWS

Serves: 16 | Preparation Time: 10 min

Cashews have a fairly neutral flavor making them the perfect partners to the bold flavors of garlic and rosemary. These cashews are so fancy, they would make tremendous gifts! No one has to know how easy they are.

Estimated Smoke Time: 30 minutes
Smoke Temp: 90°F
Try these wood chips: Apple or cherry

Ingredients:

Nuts	Brine	Finishing
❑ 1 lb raw cashews	❑ 4 cups water, room temperature ❑ ¼ cup Kosher salt	❑ 3 Tbsp melted butter ❑ 3 tsp dark brown sugar ❑ 1 tsp table salt ❑ ½ tsp ground rosemary ❑ ½ tsp garlic powder

Preparation:
1. In a medium-sized non-reactive bowl, mix water and salt until salt dissolves.
2. Add nuts and allow them to soak for 10 minutes.
3. Arrange the nuts on a sheet tray.
4. Preheat the smoker to 90°F

Smoking:
1. Smoke the nuts for 30 minutes.

Finishing:
1. In a large bowl, combine finishing ingredients.
2. Add smoked nuts and stir to combine.
3. Bake at 375°F for 15-20 minutes, stirring frequently.
4. Allow the nuts to cool completely before serving.

COLD SMOKED SALMON

Makes: 2-3 lbs cold smoked salmon |
Preparation Time: Active - 10 minutes; Passive - 30-52 hours

The only significant difference between cold smoked salmon and gravlax is the smoke. Gravlax is a Norwegian dish of raw salmon cured with salt, sugar, and dill. In our case, this cold smoked salmon recipe takes gravlax and applies a light smoke. For all intents and purposes, the salmon is still raw and should be treated as such.

Estimated Smoke Time: 12 hours
Smoke Temp: 80°F
Try these wood chips: Alder, Pecan

Ingredients:

Meat	Cure
❑ 2-3 lbs fresh salmon filet	❑ 1 ½ cups kosher salt
	❑ 1 ½ cups white sugar
	❑ 2 Tbsp fresh dill, chopped

Preparation:
1. Remove any pin bones from the salmon filet.
2. Mix cure ingredient in a small bowl.
3. Spread 1/3 of the cure in the bottom of a glass 9" x 13" pan.
4. Lay the salmon filet on top of the cure, skin side down. The cure should extend ½ inch beyond the salmon filet.
5. Spread the remaining cure on top, completely covering the salmon.
6. Cover the dish with plastic wrap and refrigerate for 24-48 hours.
7. Gently rinse the salmon and place in clean, cold water for 30 minutes.
8. Pat the salmon dry and arrange it, skin side down, on a rack over a sheet tray.
9. Refrigerate the salmon for 4 hours to dry out.

Smoking:
1. Preheat the smoker to 80°F.
2. Place the salmon directly on the smoker grates, skin side down.
3. Smoked the salmon for 12 hours.
4. Refrigerate the salmon, wrapped tightly in plastic for at least 4 hours before serving.

SMOKED VEGETABLES

Serves: 4 | **Preparation Time:** 10 min

Smoking vegetables won't drastically alter the texture (unless we're talking about tomatoes), but it will change the flavor. Any vegetable will work for this method. You are only limited by your imagination.

Estimated Smoke Time: 20 minutes for a light smoke flavor

Smoke Temp: 100°F

Try these wood chips: Any fruit wood

Ingredients:

Vegetables	Rub
❑ 1 zucchini, sliced into 1 inch rounds	❑ 1 recipe Rosemary Garlic Rub
❑ 1 lb button mushrooms	
❑ 1 yellow squash, sliced into 1 inch rounds	
❑ 1 red pepper, cut into 1 inch chunks	
❑ 1 onion, cut into 1 inch chunks	

Preparation:
1. Season the vegetables with the Rosemary Garlic Rub.
2. Place in a shallow aluminum pan.
3. Preheat the smoker to 100°F.

Smoking:
1. Smoke the vegetables for 20 minutes.

Finishing:
1. Place the vegetables straight into a preheated 400°F oven for 25-30 minutes.

COLD SMOKED TOMATO SALSA

Serves: 6 | **Preparation Time:** 5 min

Fresh salsa can't be beat. Smoked tomato salsa takes all of the delicious flavor of salsa and adds a smoky undertone, making it the perfect starter for any meal.

Estimated Smoke Time: 20 minutes
Smoke Temp: 100°F
Try these wood chips: Fruit woods

Ingredients:

Vegetables	Seasonings
❑ 4 large beefsteak tomatoes (or 6 Roma tomatoes) ❑ 2 cloves garlic, whole ❑ 1 small onion, quartered ❑ 1 jalapeno, split lengthwise and seeded	❑ 2 Tbsp fresh lime juice ❑ 1 Tbsp chopped cilantro ❑ ½ tsp salt

Preparation:
1. Place vegetables in a shallow roasting pan.
2. Preheat the smoker to 100°F.

Smoking:
1. Smoke vegetables for 20 minutes.

Finishing:
1. Place vegetables in a food processor and pulse until combined.
2. Gently stir in cilantro, lime juice, and salt.
3. Serve with tortilla chips.

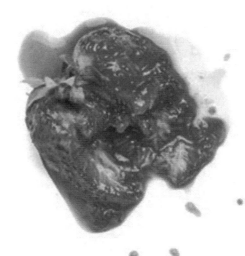

SMOKED CABBAGE STEAKS WITH DIJON VINAIGRETTE

Serves: 6 | **Preparation Time:** 5 min

Cabbage is one of the most under-utilized vegetables around. So often, this tasty veggie is relegated to coleslaw (which we love) but smoking brings out cabbage's inherent sweetness.

Estimated Smoke Time: 20 minutes
Smoke Temp: 100°F
Try these wood chips: Fruit woods

Smoked Vegetables

Ingredients:

Vegetables	Dressing
❏ 1 head of cabbage, cut into 1-inch steaks	❏ 1 shallot, finely diced ❏ ¼ cup extra-virgin olive oil ❏ 2 Tbsp fresh lemon juice ❏ 1 tsp Dijon mustard ❏ ½ tsp salt

Preparation:
1. Place vegetables in a shallow roasting pan.
2. Preheat the smoker to 100°F.

Smoking:
1. Smoke vegetables for 20 minutes.

Finishing:
1. Brush both sides of the cabbage with vegetable oil and place on a preheated grill. Grill for 2 minutes on each side.
2. In a small bowl, whisk together mustard, shallot, lemon juice, salt and olive oil.
3. Remove the cabbage from the grill and drizzle with the vinaigrette.
4. Serve immediately

DESSERTS

CALYPSO BANANA SPLITS

SMOKED FIGS WITH MASCARPONE

SMOKED PINEAPPLE WITH HONEY

NUTELLA S'MORES DIP

Desserts:

The smoker seems like an unlikely appliance for desserts. From fruit to chocolate, it is actually the perfect tool to have in your dessert arsenal.

CALYPSO BANANA SPLITS

Serves: 4 | Preparation Time: 15 min

When the summer sun is high in the sky, it's natural to want a cold treat to cool you down. The dark rum, sugar, and lime turn these delicious bananas into an exotic dessert. Add cold scoops of vanilla ice cream, and you have a winner of a dessert.

Smoke Time: 30 Mins
Smoke Temp: 100°F
Try these Wood Chips: Fruit woods

Ingredients:

Fruit	Caramel Sauce
❏ 2 firm bananas ❏ 2 Tbsp lime juice	❏ 1/3 cup brown sugar ❏ 1/3 cup dark rum ❏ ¼ cup (½ stick) butter ❏ 1 tsp ground cinnamon

Preparation:
1. Preheat the smoker to 100°F
2. Split the bananas lengthwise and brush with lime juice.

Smoking:
1. Place the bananas directly on the smoker grates, skin side down.
2. Smoke the bananas for 30 minutes, set aside.

Finishing:
1. In a large skillet, melt butter and brown sugar together until sugar is dissolved.
2. Add dark rum and allow the mixture to cook until the alcohol has burned off, about 2 minutes. Add the cinnamon.
3. Remove the skins of the one banana and place in the bottom of a bowl. Top with ½ cup of vanilla ice cream and a few spoonfuls of the rum caramel sauce. Garnish with toasted coconut, macadamia nuts, or diced pineapple.
4. Serve immediately.

SMOKED FIGS WITH MASCARPONE

Serves: 4 | Preparation Time: 10 min

Smoky, sweet figs with creamy mascarpone cheese make the perfect ending to any meal. If you cannot find fresh figs, smoke dry figs in their place and fill with the mascarpone mixture for a sweet, chewy nibble.

Estimated Smoke Time: 10 minutes
Smoke Temp: 150°F
Try these wood chips: Alder

Ingredients:

Fruit	Mascarpone Mixture
❑ 8 figs ❑ 2 Tbsp brown sugar	❑ 6 oz mascarpone cheese ❑ 1/3 cup sugar ❑ 1 orange, zested and juiced

Preparation:
1. Split each fit in half.
2. Dip the fig halves, cut side down, in brown sugar and arrange them on a sheet tray.
3. Preheat the smoker to 150°F.
4. In a small bowl, combine mascarpone, sugar, orange juice and orange zest and combine until smooth. Set aside at room temperature.

Smoking:
1. Place the sheet tray with the figs in the smoker and smoke for 10 minutes.

Finishing:
1. Place two figs in the bottom of each bowl. Top with mascarpone mixture and serve.

SMOKED PINEAPPLE WITH HONEY

Serves: 6 | **Preparation Time:** 10 min

Every "Brazilian grill" restaurant has roasted pineapple on the menu. It is the one thing we always have room for, no matter how much meat we have eaten. The kiss of smoke in this pineapple is reminiscent of those restaurants, without the meat sweats.

Estimated Smoke Time: 10 minutes
Smoke Temp: 150°F
Try these wood chips: Fruit Wood

Ingredients:

Fruit	Drizzle
❏ 1 whole, fresh pineapple	❏ 2 limes, zested and juiced ❏ ¼ cup honey

Preparation:
1. Cut the top and bottom from the pineapple and stand it on its bottom.
2. Using a sharp knife, remove the outer skin from the pineapple.
3. Cut the pineapple into six spears, removing the most fibrous part of the core.
4. Arrange pineapple spears onto a small sheet tray.
5. Preheat the smoker to 150°F.
6. In a small bowl, combine honey, lime juice and lime zest.

Smoking:
1. Smoke the pineapple spears in their sheet tray for 10 minutes.

Finishing:
1. Arrange the pineapple on a platter and drizzle with the honey-lime mixture. Serve.

NUTELLA S'MORES DIP

Serves: 4 | **Preparation Time:** 5 min

Nothing completes an outdoor dinner quite like s'mores, except this unbelievable s'mores dip. All of the flavor, none of the hassle of flaming marshmallows and unmelted chocolate.

Estimated Smoke Time: 30 minutes

Smoke Temp: 110°F

Try these wood chips: Alder

Ingredients:

Dip	Garnishes
❏ 10 ounces semi-sweet chocolate chips	❏ Graham Crackers
❏ 1 cup miniature marshmallows	❏ Banana chunks
❏ ¼ cup Nutella	❏ Strawberries
	❏ Large chunks of fresh pineapple

Preparation:

1. In an oven-safe dish, place nutella and chocolate chips.
2. Preheat smoker to 110°F.
3. Arrange garnishes on a platter.

Smoking:

1. Smoke chocolate for 15 minutes or until the chocolate chips have melted. Stir together.
2. Remove chocolate from the smoker and top with miniature marshmallows.
3. Continue to smoke for 15 minutes more until the marshmallows have melted.
4. Serve immediately with garnishes.

SIDES & APPS

ALLIGATOR EGGS

SMOKED CAESAR SALAD

KIMCHI COLESLAW

BACON & ENDIVE SALAD

SMOKED POTATO SALAD

BURNT END BAKED BEANS

ALLIGATOR EGGS

Serves: 6 | **Preparation Time:** 15 min

This cheesy, spicy appetizer contains neither alligator, nor eggs. Instead, they are named for their shape.

Estimated Smoke Time: 30 minutes
Smoke Temp: 275°F
Try these wood chips: Any

Ingredients:
- ❏ 12 thin slices bacon
- ❏ 8 ounces cream cheese, softened
- ❏ 6 jalapenos
- ❏ 1 cup sharp cheddar cheese

Preparation:
1. Slice jalapenos in half and remove seeds. Set aside.
2. In a small bowl, combine cheddar cheese and cream cheese until mixed.
3. Stuff 2 Tbsp of the cream cheese mixture into each jalapeno half.
4. Wrap each jalapeno half in one strip of bacon, securing with a toothpick.
5. Place jalapenos on a sheet tray.
6. Preheat the smoker to 275°F.

Smoking:
1. Smoke the alligator eggs on the sheet tray for 30 minutes or until the bacon is crisp. Serve immediately.

SMOKED CAESAR SALAD

Serves: 6 | **Preparation Time:** 10 min

Cold smoking the romaine lettuce adds a little something special to an ordinary Caesar salad. And skip the store bought croutons, homemade are so much better.

Estimated Smoke Time: 10 minutes
Smoke Temp: 80°F
Try these wood chips: Pecan

Ingredients:

Vegetables	Garnishes
❑ 2 heads romaine lettuce, split lengthwise in half	**Dressing:** ❑ 3 garlic cloves ❑ 3 anchovy fillets ❑ 2 lemons, juiced ❑ 1 cup grated Parmesan cheese ❑ 2 Tbsp Dijon mustard ❑ Extra-virgin olive oil ❑ Kosher salt **Croutons:** ❑ 4 slices day old Italian bread, cubed ❑ 2 Tbsp olive oil ❑ Kosher Salt & Black Pepper to taste ❑ 2 Tbsp shredded Parmesan cheese

Preparation:
1. In a blender or food processor, combine dressing ingredients, minus olive oil and salt.
2. Gradually stream in olive oil until the dressing reaches your desired consistency.
3. Taste and season with salt, if necessary.
4. Preheat oven to 400°F.
5. Toss bread cubes with olive oil, a pinch of salt and a pinch of black pepper.
6. Bake the bread for 8-10 minutes or until golden brown.
7. Preheat the smoker to 80°F.

Smoking:
1. Place romaine halves directly on the smoker's grate and smoke for 10 minutes.

Finishing:
1. Remove the romaine from the smoker and cut into bite sized pieces.
2. Toss lettuce with dressing, croutons, and shredded Parmesan. Serve immediately.

KIMCHI COLESLAW

Serves: 6 | Preparation Time: 20 min

Kimchi is a spicy Korean condiment that is typically made of cabbage and hot peppers, packed into a jar, and buried in the backyard to ferment. This slaw has a lot of the same flavors, but none of the fermentation.

Estimated Smoke Time: 10 minutes
Smoke Temp: 80°F
Try these wood chips: Alder

Ingredients:

Vegetables	Dressing
❏ 5 scallions, finely sliced	❏ ½ cup vegetable oil
❏ 1 head Napa cabbage, cut in half lengthwise	❏ ¼ cup rice wine vinegar
❏ 1 English cucumber, julienned	❏ 2 Tbsp sambal
	❏ 1 tsp salt

Preparation:

1. Preheat smoker to 80°F.
2. In a large bowl, combine rice wine vinegar, sambal, and salt and stream in oil while whisking the dressing.
3. Add scallions and cabbage but do not toss.

Smoking:

1. Place cabbage halves directly on the smoker grates and smoke for 10 minutes.

Finishing:

1. Thinly slice the cabbage and add to the dressing mixture.
2. Toss the salad together and allow it to sit for 20-30 minutes before serving.

Sides & Apps

BACON & ENDIVE SALAD

Serves: 6 | **Preparation Time:** 30 min

Bitter endive with bacon and candied walnuts? Yes, please! You'll be even more surprised by little nuggets of dried cranberries running through this delicious salad.

Estimated Smoke Time: 10 minutes
Smoke Temp: 80°F
Try these wood chips: Alder

Sides & Apps

Ingredients:

From This Book	Other
❑ Bacon Candy	❑ 2 heads endive
❑ Candied Walnuts	❑ 2 cups frisee
	❑ 1 bunch spinach, cleaned and stems removed
	❑ ¼ cup dried cranberries
	Dressing:
	❑ ¼ cup olive oil
	❑ 2 Tbsp Dijon Mustard
	❑ 1 Tbsp honey
	❑ 1 shallot, finely minced
	❑ The juice of 1 lemon
	❑ Kosher salt and fresh cracked pepper to taste

Preparation:
1. Cut the heads of endive in half, set aside.
2. Preheat smoker to 80°F.
3. In the bottom of a large bowl, combine mustard, honey, shallot, lemon juice and olive oil. Season with salt and pepper.
4. Add frisee, spinach, cranberries, bacon candy, and walnuts.

Smoking:
1. Arrange the endive directly on the smoker grates.
2. Smoke for 10 minutes and remove.

Finishing:
1. Slice the endive into thin strips and add to the rest of the salad.
2. Toss and serve.

SMOKED POTATO SALAD

Serves: 8 | **Preparation Time:** 1 hour

This traditional potato salad is amped up with a little smoked potato. The trick is to let the potatoes smoke with your meat and allow them to cool completely before assembling.

Estimated Smoke Time: 1 ½-2 hours
Smoke Temp: 275°F
Try these wood chips: Pecan

Ingredients:

Salad	Dressing
❏ 4 large baking potatoes	❏ ½ cup mayonnaise
❏ 4 large eggs, hard boiled and finely chopped	❏ The juice of 1 lemon
❏ 2 scallions, finely chopped	❏ ½ tsp black pepper
❏ 2 large dill pickles, finely chopped	❏ ½ tsp celery seed
❏ 1 rib celery, finely diced	❏ ½ tsp dried dill

Preparation:
1. Scrub potatoes.
2. Preheat the smoker to 275°F

Smoking:
1. Place the potatoes directly on the grates of the smoker and cook until tender.
2. Chill the potatoes in the fridge for 30 minutes.

Assembly:
1. In a large bowl, combine dressing ingredients.
2. Peel and cut potatoes into small cubes. Add to dressing
3. Add remaining salad ingredients and toss to combine.

BURNT END BAKED BEANS

Serves: 8 | **Preparation Time:** 30 min

The end pieces of a smoked brisket are generally known as "burnt ends". This is a bit of a misnomer since they aren't actually burnt. Instead, they are full of smoky, meaty goodness - the perfect addition to baked beans.

Estimated Smoke Time: 2 hour
Smoke Temp: 275°F
Try these wood chips: Mesquite, Hickory

Ingredients:

From This Book	Other Ingredients
❏ 8 ounces Smoked Bacon, finely diced	❏ 2 15-ounce cans of pinto beans, drained and rinsed
❏ 2 cups Quick Barbecue Sauce	❏ 3 cloves garlic, finely chopped
❏ 2 cups burnt ends from Smoked Brisket, finely chopped	❏ 1 onion, finely diced
	❏ 1 cup chicken broth
	❏ ¼ cup honey
	❏ 2 Tbsp brown sugar
	❏ Salt & Pepper to taste

Preparation:
1. Place bacon in a large, cold skillet and turn the heat on low.
2. When the bacon begins to crisp, add onion and garlic and cook until vegetables are translucent.
3. In a disposable aluminum pan, combine onion and bacon mixture, barbecue sauce, burnt ends, beans, broth, honey and brown sugar.
4. Preheat smoker to 275°F.

Smoking:
1. Smoke the beans for 2 hours, stirring once halfway through. Serve hot.

Tip: These beans can be cooked in a 350°F for 1 hour oven or in a slow cooker on low for 4-6 hours.

Made in the USA
San Bernardino, CA
02 December 2016